# 2
# by Zero

*Screenplay - English version based on 'Do Bata Shunya'*

**Dr Sanjeew Kumar Chowdhary**

**Ukiyoto Publishing**

All global publishing rights are held by

**Ukiyoto Publishing**

Published in 2023

Copyright © Dr Sanjeew Kumar Chowdhary

ISBN 9789360169848

*All rights reserved.*
*No part of this publication may be reproduced,*
*transmitted, or stored in a retrieval system, in*
*any form by any means, electronic, mechanical,*
*photocopying, recording or otherwise, without the*
*prior permission of the publisher.*

*The moral rights of the author have been asserted.*

*This is a work of fiction. Names, characters, businesses,*
*places, events, locales, and incidents are either the*
*products of the author's imagination or used in a*
*fictitious manner. Any resemblance to actual persons,*
*living or dead, or actual events is purely coincidental.*

*This book is sold subject to the condition that it shall*
*not by way of trade or otherwise, be lent, resold, hired*
*out or otherwise circulated, without the publisher's*
*prior consent, in any form of binding or cover other*
*than that in which it is published.*

www.ukiyoto.com

# Contents

| | |
|---|---:|
| Scene 1 | 1 |
| Scene 2 | 7 |
| Scene 3 | 15 |
| Scene 4 | 23 |
| Scene 5 | 32 |
| Scene 6 | 38 |
| Scene 7 | 49 |
| Scene 8 | 55 |
| Scene 9 | 65 |
| Scene 10 | 70 |
| Scene 11 | 76 |
| Scene 12 | 85 |
| Scene 13 | 93 |
| Scene 14 | 101 |
| Scene 15 | 108 |
| Scene 16 | 114 |
| Scene 17 | 119 |
| Scene 18 | 126 |
| Scene 19 | 131 |
| Scene 20 | 136 |
| Scene 21 | 142 |
| Scene 22 | 149 |
| Scene 23 | 154 |

| | |
|---|---:|
| Scene 24 | 159 |
| Scene 25 | 163 |
| Scene 26 | 172 |
| Scene 27 | 179 |
| Scene 28 | 187 |
| Scene 29 | 196 |
| Scene 30 | 206 |
| Scene 31 | 215 |
| Scene 32 | 223 |
| Scene 33 | 230 |
| Scene 34 | 239 |
| Scene 35 | 249 |
| Scene 36 | 257 |
| Scene 37 | 267 |
| Scene 38 | 276 |
| Scene 39 | 285 |
| Scene 40 | 292 |
| Scene 41 | 300 |
| Scene 42 | 309 |
| Scene 43 | 316 |
| Scene 44 | 326 |
| Scene 45 | 337 |

# Scene 1

**INT. SMALL ROOM IN A RENTED HOUSE - PUNAICHAK, PATNA - DAY**

CAMERA panning over gathering of women singing songs to the beat of a DHOLAK. The atmosphere is subdued, not particularly festive.

Now, CAMERA focuses on a 6 days old baby, KALU, who is the center of attention.

Then CAMERA shifts on to

NAYANTARA, the mother, who is busy with preparations of halwa, a sweet dish, for the 6th day ceremony of child birth.

Then CAMERA moves towards DAYA PRASAD, the father, who is sitting outside in the lobby with friends.

**NEIGHBOR SHANTI**

(Shouting)

Where are you, Nayantara? Don't delay in worshiping Chhathi. It's already 7o'clock in the evening!

**BASUKI DEVI**

(Chattering)

Now you will be spared by providing us snacks only . Otherwise, if you delay, you will have to serve us full meal.

**NAYANTARA**

(Stomping her feet)

What do you say, Amma of Bhulan! I have to take care of everything alone and unlike others none to help me.

**BASUKI DEVI**(sheepishly)

That way you are lucky otherwise if sister in law would have come here, atleast a gold jwellery would have been the cost.

Then, all women start laughing and get busy with rituals, singing songs.

Outside, Daya Prasad's friends congratulate him on arrival of his second son.

**Santosh Babu**

As you are in profit, you should have thrown cocktail party.

**AWADHESH BABU**

Now what is the matter of profit or loss in this?

**SRIDHAR BABU**

Earlier there was a son, whose dowry amount would be spent on the marriage of the second child, a daughter. Now after the arrival of this extra son, the money that'll be received in his dowry would be pure profit, wouldn't it?

Laughter. The conversation continues with jokes and teasing.

**INT. SMALL ROOM - NIGHT**

The sixth day worship is over.

**Shanti**

Now it's time to name the Child. Nayantara Ji! How will you like to call him?

NAYANTARA names the child KALU.

**NAYANTARA:** As he is jet black, Kalu will be only appropriate name for the kid.

Guests start leaving after finishing halwa served to them.

BINDU, 9, and NEERAJ, 6, take care of Kalu, showing love and affection.

**INT. KITCHEN - NIGHT**

Nayantara cooks dinner, grumbling. Daya Babu and the children are busy with the gifts, writing down names and amounts.

**BINDU**

Why at all, jotting down names with amount presented?

**DAYA BABU**

It's customary to repay the same amount back during eachother's celebration.

**INT. SMALL ROOM - NIGHT**

Everyone settles down to sleep, tired from the day's events.

**INT. SMALL ROOM - DAY (LATER)**

Neeraj and Bindu play with Kalu, taking care of him. Nayantara and Daya Babu go about their daily routines, occasionally playing with Kalu.

Kalu pees while in father's lap and Daya Babu starts calling mother Nayantara to clean the mess.

**NAYANTARA (murmuring to herself)**

Everyone enjoys playing with the child, but everyone's grandmother dies cleaning the mess, as if it is only my responsibility.

**DAYA BABU**

(Ignoring, wise)

...

They continue their lives, accepting their roles and responsibilities, finding joy in their new child.

**FADE TO BLACK**

❑❑

# Scene 2

**INT. SAME ROOM OF RENTED HOUSE - PUNAICHAK, PATNA - DAY (SIX MONTHS LATER)**

Camera focuses on the 6 months old baby Kalu.

KALU, now stout and nicknamed MOTU HALWAI, is growing quickly. DAYA PRASAD boasts about his son's development.

**DAYA PRASAD**

You guys will see, this promising son will start walking before nine months.

**DISSOLVE TO:**

**INT. SAME ROOM - DAY (LATER)**

KALU falls ill with diarrhea, becoming weak. NAYANTARA loses hope, but Daya Prasad insists on trying everything, including medical treatment and superstitions.

**DR. LALA SURYAVANSHAM**

There is very little chance of survival. If you allow me, then only I can just try to do my best

**NAYANTARA**

(With tears)

If it is so, then leave it to God's will.

**DAYA PRASAD**

No sir, you try your best. I am sure, God will not let us down.

**DISSOLVE TO:**

### EXT. DANAPUR - DAY

Nayantara takes KALU to a popular highly esteemed AUGHAD BABA, who ties a talisman on Kalu's arm.

**AUGHAD BABA**

If this talisman is not returned to me by tomorrow, then your child will be saved, otherwise God is the master.

**DISSOLVE TO:**

**EXT. DANAPUR – NEXT DAY**

**NAYANTARA**(rushing towards Aughad Baba anxiously)

Baba! Baba! Is talisman with you? It's not on Kalu's arm.

**AUGHAD BABA**

Don't worry, Amma! It has not come back to me. It's some where in your house.The Child will definitely recover and live long.

**DISSOLVE TO:**

**INT. RENTED HOUSE – MONTAGE**

KALU recovers slowly, starts walking after two years. The family grows, moving to a government bungalow. A scooter in the verandah symbolizes prosperity.

**DISSOLVE TO:**

**INT.GOVT.BUNGALOW-DAY(5YRS. LATER)**

KALU, now 5yrs old, is ignored by the family, often left alone while all members going to visit tourist places. He dreams of visiting those places, details of which he hears about from his brothers.

**SOHAN**

(Comforting)

No problem, Kalu! Next time uncle and aunt will really take you with them. Then we will hear more funny stories from you.

**DISSOLVE TO:**

**EXT. STREET - DAY (HOLI FESTIVAL)**

Kids spraying colours on each other with their parents around.

Someone paints Kalu's face with black colour.

KALU is teased for his dark complexion. His mother, NAYANTARA, laughs with others, unaware of the impact on her son.

**NEIGHBORING AUNT**

Why did you paint unnecessarily? He is already completely black, then why to waste color?

Every one laughs. Kalu appears ashamed and disappointed.

**DISSOLVE TO:**

**INT.GOVT.BUNGALOW - EVENING**

**KALU**

(Applying gulal to Nayantara's feet avoiding touch)

Mother, I was afraid that your white feet might be stained by the touch of my black hands.

Annoyed Nayantara tries to slap Kalu

**DAYA PRASAD**

(Interrupting Nayantara's slap)

Instead of getting angry at the innocence of this innocent child, we should understand our mistake.

Nayantara hugs Kalu, realizing her mistake.

**DISSOLVE TO:**

**EXT. KHANNA'S UNCLE'S HOUSE - EVENING**

> **Holi celebration by applying gulal to each other.**

**MONIKA** (teasing KALU)

Kalu! You came so late. Now, you will miss the snacks. Your favourite Kachori finished.

Aunty serves Snacks to Kalu ahead of all kids.

KALU enjoys kachoris and curds, teasing Monika.

**KHANNA JI** (affectionately holding Kalu by his side after applying gulal on his forehead)

See this genius boy. He is too good in every field and all kids should take inspiration from him.

Kalu wants to stay longer and play with Monika.

He's brought back by his elder brother, NEERAJ.

**NEERAJ**

(Excusing the delay)

Come on, we have to go back to home before it's too late. Otherwise mother will be angry.

**FADE TO BLACK.**

**Note:** This chapter introduces new complexities in Kalu's life, including his illness, recovery, and the growing family's dynamics. The screenplay captures the essence of these events and the emotional journey of the characters.

❏❏

# Scene 3

**INT. GOVERNMENT BUNGALOW - GARDANIBAGH, PATNA - MORNING**

Camera panning over a government bungalow focuses on Kalu.

KALU, age 6, is excited to go to school for the first time. DAYA PRASAD is apprehensive but supportive.

**DAYA PRASAD**

(To Kalu)

Ready for your first day, my boy?

**KALU**

Yes, Papa! I can't wait!

**DISSOLVE TO: FLASH BACK**

**INT. SCHOOL CLASSROOM - DAY (ONE YEAR BEFORE)**

Kids giving ENTRANCE TEST

KALU refuses to write anything in the entrance exam. Teacher offers him toffey but he refuses to take any.

**KALU** (sobbing)

No, no! I'll not study here. I am comfortable with study at home. My mother teaches me best.

NAYANTARA is proud of his stubbornness. She hugs him showering lots of love.

**NAYANTARA**

(To Kalu)

You'll study only from me? That's my boy! I am proud of you, mamma's son.

**DISSOLVE TO:**

**EXT. SCHOOL GATE - DAY (LATER)**

KALU waves happily as he starts formal studies directly from the second class. He excels in his studies.

**DISSOLVE TO:**

**INT. NEW SCHOOL - DAY (AFTER FOURTH STANDARD)**

KALU's old school closes, and he joins a prestigious middle-class school with English nomenclature. He becomes everyone's favorite.

**PRINCIPAL**

(To Kalu)

Would you like to study in our school? Hope you like our school.

**KALU**

(Excitedly)

Yes, ma'am!

**DISSOLVE TO:**

**INT. CLASSROOM - DAY (after 6 months)**

Class Teacher Miss Mary handing over report cards to students.

**MISS MARY**

Good morning, Students! As you all have your results of half yearly exam. Most of you have done well. A few who could not do good this time, should not be disappointed. Do more labour from now on and pass the annual exam in flying colours. I am happy to announce that Mr Kalika Prasad have topped the list. Congratulations to him. Now he will be monitor of your class instead of Miss Manjula.

**ALL STUDENTS**

Congratulations, Kalika!

**KALIKA**(Kalu)

Thanks Ma'am! Thanks all. I'll try my best to maintain peace and harmony in the class with your help and to fulfill my responsibility as monitor.

**MANJULA** (after Teacher leaves the class)

It's not fair. You got extra favour from Miss Mary. I'll not continue in this school now and move to another one in a month.

**KALU** (trying to pacify Manjula)

Please don't be so disappointed. It's just half yearly exam and you may be topper in the final exam.

Manjula leaves classroom stomping her feet.

KALU moves to a government high school after repeating the same result in final exam. He walks to school with his friend VINOD.

**DISSOLVE TO:**

**EXT. NEIGHBORHOOD - EVENING**

KALU plays with friends, including MONIKA. He sneaks into the group of girls, enjoying their company.

**OLDER CHILD**

(To Kalu)

Why are you playing with the girls?

**MONIKA**

(Defending Kalu)

He's our friend! Leave him alone.

**DISSOLVE TO:**

**INT. KHANNA SAHIB'S HOUSE - DAY (BIRTHDAY PARTY)**

After blowing out candle Monika cuts the cake with her parents by her side. Every one present claps, singing Birthday Song.

**MONIKA** (pulling Kalu by his arm)

Please come with me for the dance.

**KALU** (hesitates)

I can't dance. I may spoil your performance too. Select some other as partner.

**MONIKA**

Don't Shy. We are going to do same Radha Krishna dance, done so many times before.

KALU and MONIKA sing and dance in a duet. Everyone claps and enjoys the performance.

**MONIKA**

(To Kalu)

Whether I win or lose, I will always choose you as my partner in future too.

**KALU**

(Shyly)

I'll try my best not to spoil your beauty.

**MONIKA**

(Giving Kalu a rose bud)

Thank you for being my partner.

**KALU**

(Handing her a hand drawn congratulation card)

Happy birthday, Monika.

**FADE TO BLACK.**

**Note:** Chapter 3 explores Kalu's educational journey, his friendships, and his growing talents. The screenplay captures his transition from a stubborn child to an excelling student and his special bond with Monika. It also hints at the economic challenges faced by his family and the contrast with the more affluent neighbors.

# Scene 4

**EXT. HIGH SCHOOL YARD - DAY**

Camera opens up panning a school yard and focuses on Kalu.

KALU, now older, gazes at the big yard and huge building of his new high school. He's nervous but excited about sports.

**VINOD**

(To Kalu)

You'll be a champion one day, I know it!

**KALU**

I'll try my best!

**VINOD**

Though you are good in many games like football, badminton, chess and cricket, I'll suggest to concentrate on one.

**KALU**

You are right. Now onwards I'll concentrate on cricket and will try to represent my school in different tournaments.

**VINOD**

Best of luck! I'm sure you will lead the school team one day.

**DISSOLVE TO:**

### INT. CLASSROOM - DAY

KALU sits in the back row with VINOD.

**KALU**

I enjoy sitting here, free to do some nusience for my own pleasure.

**VINOD**

But soon you will be moved to the front bench, as you'll excel in the exam and will be appointed as class monitor.

**VINOD Imitates as CLASS TEACHER**

(To Kalu)

Well done, Kalu! You're our new class monitor.

**DISSOLVE TO:**

**EXT. ROAD-SIDE PLAYGROUND - DAY**

KALU's skill in sports, especially cricket, improves. He also plays traditional street games and girls' games, becoming popular among the girls.

**NEIGHBORHOOD WOMAN**

(To her child)

Look at Kalu, always reading and playing well too. Be like him!

**DISSOLVE TO:**

**EXT. SIDE OF THE ROAD - DAY**

KALU accidentally hits a NEIGHBOR AUNTY with a cricket ball. She slaps him and complains to his parents.

**NEIGHBOR AUNTY**

(Angrily)

You children are a menace! Your ball is seized and I'll complain to your parents.

**KALU**

(Apologies)

Sorry Aunty! Not done deliberately. Please forgive. Will never repeat the mistake.

**All CHILDREN**

Please Aunty! Please

Aunty refuses to oblige.


**DISSOLVE TO:**

**INT. KALU'S HOUSE - EVENING**

KALU is punished and feels lonely. His friends refuse to play with him.

**FRIEND**

(To Kalu)

Either You have to get back the ball from Aunty or buy a new ball. Otherwise we won't allow you to play with us.

**KALU**

She will not budge and from where I can get money to buy a new ball. Don't be unfair to me. We are friends and it could happen to anyone of us. All of us should contribute and can easily buy a new ball.

**ONE FRIEND**

He's right. It's not his fault. We should not play by roadside and from now on will always play in playground.

**ANOTHER FRIEND**

No, it's final. If he will not bring the ball, we will not allow him to play with us.

**KALU**

(Desperate)

I'll find a way!

**DISSOLVE TO:**

**INT. KALU'S HOUSE - LATER**

KALU breaks BINDU's piggy bank and takes money. He replaces it with a new one, thinking he's clever.

**BINDU**

(Confronting Kalu)

You took my money, didn't you?

**KALU**

(Defensively)

No, I borrowed it from Monika!

**DISSOLVE TO:**

**INT. SAME HOUSE - EVENING**

**BINDU**

(to Monika)

Have you lent any money to Kalu?

**MONIKA**

(After looking at KALU'S face)

Yes, I have. What happened, Didi? Is it wrong to help your friend in need? He has promised to repay back at his convenience.

**BINDU**

(To Kalu)

Ok, Fine! This time she has saved you. Never do it again.

**KALU**

(With Remorse facie)

Sorry, Didi! I'll never borrow in future.

**KALU**

(To Monika)

Thanks, MONIKA!

**KALU**

(Talking to himself)

It's worse! Now Monika knows that I am a lier. She saved me but what about my image! It got tarnished today. I'll never steal anything in future.

**EXT. PLAYGROUND- DAY (LATER)**

KALU plays cricket passionately, improving his game. He's filled with remorse but soon forgets and gains confidence.

**VINOD**

(To Kalu)

You're getting better every day!

**KALU**

(Smiling)

I'm just getting started!

**FADE TO BLACK.**

**Note:** Chapter 4 delves into Kalu's growth as a student and athlete, his popularity among friends, and his struggle with moral dilemmas. The screenplay captures his transition from a shy boy to a confident young man, highlighting his passion for cricket and his complex relationship with his peers and family.

# Scene 5

**EXT. SCHOOL GROUNDS - DAY**

Camera opens up panning over a group of students and later focuses on Kalu.

Students surround KALIKA (KALU), celebrating his top score in the school. RAHUL proposes a party.

**RAHUL**

Kalika, you've come first among all sections of Patna High School! Party time!

**KALIKA (KALU)**

(Laughing)

We'll have a feast, but patience, my friends! the fruit of waiting is sweet.

VINOD approaches, announcing his father's transfer to Ranchi. They share a tearful goodbye.

**VINOD**

Maybe we'll never meet again.

**KALIKA (KALU)**

No, destiny will bring us together again. We won't say goodbye.

**DISSOLVE TO:**

**INT. KALU'S HOUSE - DAY**

KALU is bored during summer vacation. RICHA, a neighbor, invites him to play.

**RICHA**

Come over, Kalu. Let's play together.

**DISSOLVE TO:**

**INT. RICHA'S BEDROOM - DAY**

RICHA attempts to seduce KALU, but he remains innocent and unaffected. She becomes angry but sends him away with chocolates fearing disclosure.

**DISSOLVE TO:**

**EXT. NEIGHBORHOOD - DAY**

SHARDA AUNTY and KHANNA AUNTY admire KALU's sweater. KHANNA AUNTY sends KALU to buy groceries.

**KHANNA AUNTY**

Take this money and buy some gram flour and salt. Hand them to Monika at my house.

**KALU**

Sure, Auntie!

**DISSOLVE TO:**

### EXT. STREET - DAY

KALU collides with a motorcycle, injuring his forehead. A KIND STRANGER takes him to the hospital and then home.

**KIND STRANGER**

(To Kalu)

You'll be okay, young man. Let me drop you home.

**DISSOLVE TO:**

### INT. KALU'S HOUSE - DAY

KALU's MOTHER, angry and worried, beats him with a stick. SHARDA AUNTY and KHANNA AUNTY intervene.

**KALU'S MOTHER**

(Angrily)

You're a worthless vagabond!

**SHARDA AUNTY**

(Defending Kalu)

Nayantara, this boy is pure gold. You're lucky to have him. I have sent him to buy some groceries and he met an accident. Instead of consoling, you are beating him badly.

**KALU'S MOTHER**

(Still angry)

You people have spoiled him!

**FADE TO BLACK.**

**Note:** Chapter 5 explores Kalu's academic success, his friendship with Vinod, and an unsettling encounter with Richa. It also highlights his innocence, his relationship with his neighbors, and a painful incident that leads to a confrontation with his mother.

This chapter introduces complex emotions and situations, and the screenplay aims to capture these nuances.

❑❑

# Scene 6

**INT. SCHOOL CRICKET TEAM MEETING - NIGHT**

Camera opens up panning over a room with teammates of cricket team sitting together and focuses on Dilip


CAPTAIN DILIP addresses the team, including KALIKA (KALU).

**CAPTAIN DILIP**

Tomorrow's our first match, and we must win. I'm choosing only senior players.

**KALIKA (KALU)**

(Defiantly)

The seed that germinates will flourish. Today is in your hands, but tomorrow will be mine. Mind it.

**CAPTAIN DILIP**

Keep your difficult literary dialogues with yourself. You're not playing tomorrow and that's final.

**DISSOLVE TO:**

**EXT. CRICKET FIELD - MORNING**

**DILIP**

(To Kalu)

Kalika! You are in the team for today's match replacing Mohit. He is having high fever today. Just try to do your best and grab this God sent opportunity.

**KALU**

Thanks, I'll try to give my hundred percent. Let's hope for the best!

The match is underway. Scoreboard showing 110 for no wicket in favour of team in opposition.

KALIKA (Kalu) approaches towards worried Captain Dilip.

**KALU**

Please give me an over to try. Anyway we are not getting wickets and batters are scoring at their will.

Dilip throws ball towards him unwillingly.

On Kalu's first ball, batsman welcomes him hitting huge six.

Kalu gets wicket with very next ball and breaks long partnership.

Dilip and other teammates pat his back.

Two balls later, again he bowls the batsman out and crowd becomes jubilant. Teammates surround him with more enthusiasm now.

Before the last ball of his over, Kalu whispers something to the wicket keeper.

When he bowls a flighted delivery outside off stump, the batsman steps out, missing completely as ball spins further away from him and he gets stumped by wicket keeper.

**COMMENTATOR**

This short thin-built new bowler Kalika has turned the game on its head taking three vital wickets in one over. Still, with long batting line up, high score of more than 250 is still on card. Let's see how things go on from here.

**DISSOLVE TO:**

**EXT. SAME CRICKET FIELD - DAY ( LATER)**

Camera opens up panning over to sideline over to Players off the field, taking lunch.

Focus of camera shifting to Scoreboard showing total score of the opposite team 172 all out.

**COMMENTRY**

(in the background)

Newcomer Kalika did the magic and got 7 wickets for 20 runs in his 6 overs preventing a big target for his team restricting the total to 172 only.

**DISSOLVE TO:**

**EXT. SAME CRICKET FIELD - AFTERNOON**

Camera opens up focussing over Kalika coming into the field from boundary line.

KALIKA walks towards pitch with bat in his left hand.

Scoreboard showing 87 for 6 for Patna High school team against Target of 173.

**COMMENTATOR**

New man coming in, is Kalika who did the magic with his ball earlier. Can he do the same during batting and take his team out of woods to win the match from this hopeless situation? This is a million dollars question today.

CAMERA in quick succession shows KALIKA hitting fours and sixes.

He performs brilliantly, leading the team to victory.

**COMMENTATOR**

And Kalika has done it! A three-wicket win! What an upset!

The team celebrates, hugging KALIKA.

**DISSOLVE TO:**

**INT. SCHOOL CRICKET TEAM MEETING - DAY**

MOHIT returns, and KALIKA is benched. He looks disappointed.

**KALU**

(To himself)

I did so well in last match but now being ignored. It happens in game and I'll not lose hope. I should continue practicing hard and with grace of God I may get further chances.

He practices harder, gets more chances, and performs well.

But his team loses in the semi-final.

**DISSOLVE TO:**

### INT. SCHOOL OFFICE - DAY

SPORTS TEACHER ZAFAR SAHEB argues with CAPTAIN DILIP and consults the PRINCIPAL.

**ZAFAR SAHEB**

(To Principal)

We need a new captain. I propose Kalika.

**PRINCIPAL**

His leadership ability is questionable. Consult the senior players.

**DISSOLVE TO:**

**INT. SCHOOL CRICKET TEAM MEETING – DAY**

**ZAFAR SIR**

(To seniors)

Dilip is no longer captain of the team as decided by the management of School. So, you can suggest one name but all of you must agree on that name.

Senior players discuss the captaincy issue but can't reach on consensus.

**ZAFAR SIR**

If you don't pick up a name among yourselves, I will suggest Kalika's name, if you all agree.

**ONE SENIOR**

But he is too junior and lacks leadership experience.

**ANOTHER SENIOR**

Sir, other way round, it's good that he is junior. He respects each one of us. He will listen to our advices without having ego problem. So, now as it will be collective leadership, we all will play really as one team.

They all agree on KALIKA as new Skipper.

**ALL SENIOR PLAYERS**

We'll help him together. We'll emerge stronger.

They inform KALIKA, who hesitates but agrees.

In comes Principal Sir.

**PRINCIPAL**

(To Kalika)

Congratulations, Captain Kalika. We have immense hope in you.

**KALIKA**

I am not alone, Sir. Each and every member of the team is Captain. Team will work on collective leadership and we believe, will do wonders.

**PRINCIPAL**

Go ahead. Well begun is half done. Best of luck to all of you.

**ALL TOGETHER**

Thanks, Sir! We will keep our and your head high bringing so many laurels to our School.

**DISSOLVE TO:**

**EXT. CRICKET FIELD - DAY - MONTAGE**

KALIKA leads the team to victory in local and state-level competitions one after another. The team lifts trophies after trophies and KALIKA's image as a hero emerges strong..

**FADE TO BLACK.**

**Note:** Chapter 6 showcases Kalika's rise from a benched player to a star performer and eventually the captain of the school cricket team. His journey is marked by determination, skill, leadership, and the ability to unite his team.

The screenplay captures the key moments of his cricketing journey, including his initial disappointment, his triumphant performance, his struggles with being benched, and his eventual rise to captaincy.

# Scene 7

**INT. KALU'S HOUSE - DAY**

Camera opens up panning over a house and moves in to a room focussing on few children getting dressed up.

Bindu, Neeraj, Shekhar, Puneet, Anupam, and Kalu are getting ready for a wedding ceremony. Kalu is dressed up by his father.

**PUNEET**

(Taunting)

The lighter colour of dress on Kalu looks pperfect, color contrast perfect!

**KALU**

(Smiling)

Thanks, Puneet, my dear!

**DISSOLVE TO:**

**INT.WEDDING CEREMONY - NIGHT**

Kalu meets his old school friend SUCHITA. They catch up on old times.

As the meal being served, Kalu's father, DAYA PRASAD, realizes Kalu is missing.

**DAYA PRASAD**

(Angrily)

Where is Sahabzade missing now?

**NAYANTARA**

(Ordering Neeraj)

Catch him and bring him back while beaten.

Neeraj finds Kalu, slaps him, and drags him back. Kalu eats silently, sobbing.

**NAYANTARA**

(Scolding)

Sit down peacefully!

Later, Kalu waves goodbye to Suchita, still feeling humiliated.

**DISSOLVE TO:**

**EXT. STREET - DAY**

Kalu learns that Vishambhar uncle is taking Neeraj bhaiya and Bindu didi to the cinema. He runs after them and catches up.

**KALU**

(Controlling his breath)

Why at all have you come here leaving me? You say, I am dearest of all to you. Then?

**VISHAMBHAR UNCLE**

(Smiling)

I searched a lot for you. Now calm down and watch the movie in peace. I'll give you all popcorn and coke.

**ALL THREE**

Thank you, Uncle! You are so nice!

**DISSOLVE TO:**

**EXT. KALU'S BACKYARD - DAY**

Kalu mimics the hero from the movie, even picking up a bidi stub and lighting it. He coughs loudly, and his father, DAYA PRASAD, catches him.

**DAYA PRASAD**

(Enraged)

What are you doing? Smoking? Idiot! You are completely spoilt child.

**KALU**

(Crying)

I will never do it again! Please apologise me.


DAYA PRASAD thrashes Kalu, who hides in a corner of the house, praying his mother doesn't find him out.

**FADE TO BLACK.**


**Note:** Chapter 7 provides a glimpse into Kalu's family life and his interactions with friends and relatives. It highlights his mischievous nature, his love for cinema, and his close relationships with family members.


The screenplay captures key moments, including a family wedding, a trip to the cinema, and Kalu's experimentation with acting and smoking, which leads to a stern lesson from his father.


These scenes help to build Kalu's character and provide context for his upbringing and the influences that shape his personality.

❏❏

# Scene 8

### INT. CLASSROOM - DAY

Camera opens up panning over the whole class and then focuses on Shatrughan collcting names of students agreeing for participation.

Names are being collected for the All India Inter School Debate Competition. SHATRUGHAN mischievously writes down Kalika's name. Kalika is surprised but goes along with it.

### INT. SCHOOL AUDITORIUM - DAY

Kalika and Shatrughan participate in the selection program. Kalika speaks without hesitation, and the applause signals him to end his speech.

**TEACHER**

Kalika and Shatrughan came first and second and so they will represent our School at district level elocution competition. Good luck to both of them.

**AUDIENCE**

Congratulations both of you, Kalika and Shatrughan!

DISSOLVE TO:

**INT. PATNA DISTRICT LEVEL COMPETITION HALL- DAY**

Kalika and Shatrughan compete among students from famous private schools.

**ONE JUDGE**

(Announcing the result)

In the junior section, there's a tie between Kalika of Patna High School and Miss Ruhi of Mount Carmel school, Patna. Even after another attempt to break the tie, we could not succeed. So, both of them will go to State level of competition at Hazaribagh.

Best of luck to all successful orators and hope you win so many prizes at state level.

Kalika handshakes with RUHI and both of them wishes good luck to each other.

**DISSOLVE TO:**

**INT. HAZARIBAGH COMPETITION HALL – DAY**

With PRINCIPAL MR. BANERJEE accompanying him, Kalika participates in competition. He clears preliminary round in flying colours and advances to final extempore round.

**ANNOUNCER**

After completion of Extempore round on topic 'Children are better than adults', we are pleased to announce that a record has been created here. For the first time, a boy from junior section has been declared 'Best speaker of the House'. He is (after a long silence) Boy from a Govt. School - Mr Kalika Prasad of Patna High School. He will get the Running Shield here and will automatically qualify for National level elocution competition to be held at Imphal, Mizoram next month.

Kalika Prasad, please come onto the dias and receive your award from Chief guest.


Kalika goes to the dias with Principal Mr Banerjee Sir and receives the Shield among thunderous applause from audience.

He hands it over to Principal Sir and touches his feet.

**KALU**

(Taking mike)

Thanks all my teachers, particularly Principal Sir, who gave me their blessings and proper guidance. I dedicate this success to my mother Mrs Nayantara Devi, my first teacher though she is only a housewife. I thank my father too, who always stood by my side and my brothers and sisters. Thanks all my dear friends without whose support I would not have achieved this.

(With folded hands looking upwards) Thanks God!

**DISSOLVE TO:**

**EXT. STREET - DAY**

MONIKA encourages Kalika and throws a peanut party.

**MONIKA**

Please don't get depressed. Your father has decided not to send you to Imphal for national competition because he loves you too much. You are too young to travel alone to such distant place and he is not able to manage leave to accompany you.

(After brief pause)

Don't underestimate this achievement. You have increased the respect in eyes of all of us.

**KALIKA**

I am overwhelmed with the happiness of coming first in the state. I have learnt a lesson from you to celebrate the present achievement without thinking of future.

Come on, let us sing and dance.

**DISSOLVE TO:**

**INT. SCHOOL - DAY**

Kalika is honored in school, and his picture is framed in the principal's office room.

**PRINCIPAL SIR**

Kalika is Pride of our school. You all love him, that's fine. But also take some inspiration from him and try to inculcate his virtues.

All students applause by clapping.

**PRINCIPAL SIR**

(To Kalu)

Kalika! Though you should be proud of your achievements but always try to remain humble and down to earth.

He promises to remain humble throughout his life.

**DISSOLVE TO:**

**INT. KALIKA'S HOUSE - DAY**

Kalika brings his half-yearly examination results and hands it over to his father.

**DAYA PRASAD**

(To Kalu)

Oh! It's no wonder that you have slipped to second position in merit list. You were not concentrating on your study these days as much as before. These days, you were more interested in extracurricular activities like cricket, oration, debate etc.

**Mother Nayantara Devi**

(Slapping on his face twice)

It's all negligence. Now on, no more wandering around with your vagabond friends and give more time to your study.

**DAYA PRASAD**

(Father, consoling)

No, no! Nothing to worry too much. It happens in life now and then that you achieve lesser than expected. Don't lose heart. Keep it up.

Perform better in the annual examination. There are some ups and downs in every one's life. Taking all in your strides, always move forward.

**NAYANTARA DEVI**

(Mother, angry)

This is sheer negligence!

Kalu hides in his usual corner, weeping bitterly, reflecting on the pressure to succeed.

**KALU**

(To himself)

I may be only child who got thrashed for getting second in the class merit list. Other's parents become too happy if he or she comes in first three. It's all because I slipped from the top. Nothing succeeds like success and all want credit for that. No body owns your failure and remains by your side. You are left alone to fight your own battle.

I will and come out stronger!

**DISSOLVE TO:**

**INT. CLASSROOM - DAY (After 6 months)**

In the annual examination, Kalika returns as the topper, but the emotional toll of the previous disappointment lingers.

**FADE TO BLACK.**

**Note:** Chapter 8 explores Kalika's growth as he enters adolescence, balancing his mischievous nature with newfound responsibilities. The chapter highlights his unexpected success in debate competitions, his relationship with his friends and family, and the pressure he feels to excel academically.

The screenplay captures key moments, including his participation in debate competitions, his celebration with friends, his interactions with his parents, and his struggle with academic expectations.

These scenes provide insight into Kalika's character, his ambitions, his relationships, and the challenges he faces as he navigates the complexities of adolescence.

❏❏

# Scene 9

**EXT. STREET - DAY**

Camera opens up panning over a street and then focuses on to Kalu and Monika.

Kalika and Monika are walking together, deep in conversation. They're close, but there's an unspoken tension between them.

**KALIKA**

Monica! These days I am little worried.

**MONIKA**

Worried about what?

**KALIKA**

About our relationship, this intimacy. Should not we give it a name?

**MONIKA**

You try to name it.

**KALU**

I don't know what to call this, Monika. It's more than friendship, but it's not love, is it?

**MONIKA**

(smiling)

Let's not give it a name, Kalu. We know what it is, and that's enough.

### INT. CLASSROOM - DAY

Kalika struggles with a new exam format. He answers the questions but is clearly unsatisfied.

### INT. NANIHAL (GRANDMOTHER'S HOUSE) - DAY

Kalika enjoys juicy mangoes, forgetting his worries during the holidays.

**INT. KALIKA'S HOUSE - DAY**

Kalika returns to find out he barely passed in first class. His PARENTS, TEACHERS, and CLASSMATES are surprised and sympathetic, but he's deeply hurt.

**INT. KALIKA'S ROOM - DAY**

Kalika sits in a dark corner, tears in his eyes, reflecting on his shattered self-image.

**EXT. STREET - DAY**

Kalika learns to ride a bicycle, falling and getting minor wounds. He faces insults and slaps while colliding with pedestrian but perseveres.

**INT. KALIKA'S HOUSE - DAY**

Mother hands over NEERAJ's short trousers and shirts to Kalika. He's excited to wear trousers for the first time and is all set to start a new chapter in life.

**EXT. COLLEGE GATE - DAY**

Kalika, now in trousers and carrying a bag, stands at the gate of Patna Science College, ready to embark on a new journey.

**FADE TO BLACK.**

**Note:** Chapter 9 delves into Kalika's relationship with Monika, a bond that defies easy categorization. It also explores Kalika's academic struggles, his shattered self-image, and his determination to move forward.

The screenplay captures these key moments, including his conversations with Monika, his struggles with a new exam format, his time at his grandmother's house, his learning to ride a bicycle, and his transition to college life.

These scenes provide insight into Kalika's emotional growth, his relationships, and his resilience as he faces new challenges and prepares for the next phase of his life.

❏❏

# Scene 10

**EXT. COLLEGE CAMPUS - DAY**

Camera opens up panning over college campus and focuses on Kalu entering through gate on bicycle.

Kalika arrives at college on his bicycle, looking lost and nervous. A GROUP OF STUDENTS misdirects him, and he ends up near the toilet. They laugh at him.

**INT. LECTURE HALL - DAY**

Kalika meets AJAY, ABHAY, and VIMAL. They become friends. The PROFESSOR introduces himself, and the students introduce themselves.

**EXT. MONIKA'S HOUSE- EVENING**

Kalika and Monika share their first-day experiences, laughing and teasing each other.

**MONIKA**

Oh fool! I am asking about friendship with any girl at college.

**KALU**

You know me, I am a tortoise, not a rabbit. What about you? Trapped any one?

**MONIKA**

I don't need any more fool. I already have one readymade.

They laugh together.

### INT. KALIKA'S ROOM - NIGHT

Kalika reflects on his clothes and mannerisms, compares his with those of fellow college students, feeling out of place.

**KALIKA**

(Talking to himself)

How modern they are in their attire, manner and attitude! We belong to an old fashioned traditional family. Are we poor? My father does not earn enough money or is he miser enough not to look after his children well? Do my parents love me as much as their? Probably no but yes, I have found often lots of love in eyes of my mother and father too. May be we are too many and that may be the root cause of our simple living.

**LATER :**

He reads biographies of great people like Gandhi, Abraham Lincoln etc. and goes through religious texts, realising value of simple living and high thinking, finds solace in simplicity.

**INT. MONIKA'S HOUSE - DAY**

Kalika watches Monika's practice dance for the college anniversary celebration. He encourages her, and their relationship deepens.

**INT. WOMEN'S COLLEGE - AUDITORIUM - NIGHT**

MONIKA'S dance performance is a hit. Kalika claps enthusiastically but feels a pang of jealousy when a HERO holds Monika's hand.

**EXT. WOMEN'S COLLEGE - NIGHT**

MONIKA introduces Kalika to her team. A FILM DIRECTOR approaches Monika and offers her a contract as a heroine. She accepts, excitedly.

**INT. KALIKA'S HOUSE - DAY**

Months later, Kalika reads Monika's letters from Mumbai, which gradually becomes less frequent. He feels a sense of loss as she moves on to her new life in Mumbai.

**INT. KALIKA'S LONELY CORNER - NIGHT**

Kalika sits in his lonely corner, reflecting on his friendship with Monika. He finds comfort in the memories and the realization that at least he had a beautiful friend like her.

**FADE TO BLACK.**

**Note:** Chapter 10 explores Kalika's transition to college life, his feelings of inadequacy, and his deepening relationship with Monika. The screenplay captures key moments, including his first day at college, his self-reflection, his support for Monika's dance practice, and Monika's success leading to her departure for Mumbai.

The chapter also highlights Kalika's emotional growth, his ability to find contentment in simplicity, and his bitter-sweet feelings as he loses his close friend to a new opportunity.

These scenes provide a rich tapestry of emotions and experiences, setting the stage for further developments in Kalika's life.

## Scene 11

**INT. MONIKA'S MUMBAI APARTMENT - DAY**

Camera opens up panning over apartment and then inside room, later focuses on Monika with her parents

Monika's parents are preparing to leave. PRODUCER-DIRECTOR NITIN has made lavish arrangements for them. Monika is nervous about her first shoot.

**MONIKA**

(To Parents)

Can you not stay for few more days with me? I have just finished my audition. I was so nervous that day though Nitin Sir was quite helpful. He took me to the studio in his grand Mercedes car and remained there till my audition was complete. Still I need your emotional support. Even Kalu is not here to help me out.

**FATHER**

We also don't want to leave you alone. Already one week has gone. I have to do my job too. Above all, we also have to look after your brother and sister. Now, be a brave girl and allow us to go back.

**MONIKA**

Ok, but keep coming frequently.


**INT. FILM STUDIO - EVENING**

Monika's first shoot. Nervous at first, later she becomes comfortable and completes the shoot successfully.

**INT. MONIKA'S APARTMENT - NIGHT**

Monika's parents leave, and she begins to feel lonely.

Nitin suggests attending late evening parties, but she resists.

### INT. NITIN'S CAR - DAY

Nitin spends time with Monika, sharing personal stories. Monika begins to give him space in her life. She starts going to party once in a while.

### INT. PARTY - NIGHT

Nitin insists Monika to try a drink. She takes a sip but refuses more.

**NITIN**

(To Monika)

This is the problem with you small town girls. This way you can't survive in film line.

**MONIKA**

(Angrily)

I have already told you before. I'll not do all these tantrums. Accept me as I am, for my work. If I lack talent, leave me. l am always ready to go back. I am comfortable with graduation study in law after finishing my plus two.

An argument ensues, and Monika leaves angrily.

**INT. MONIKA'S APARTMENT- DAY**

Nitin apologizes but pushes Monika to accept the film world's ways. Monica stands firm on her ground, and a heated exchange reveals Nitin's true intentions.

**MONIKA**

Today you are convincing me to take liquor. Later on you will say that it is normal practice here to share bed now and then with strangers.

**NITIN**

What is wrong in this? After all you are grown adult. Sex is just like taking foods and a taste change is always welcome in both.

**MONIKA**

You Monster! Now I realise your true intention. I am leaving your filthy world right now.

**NITIN**

No, you can't do this. You have signed a contract with me. I can sue you.

**MONIKA**

To hell with your contact. Leave at once or I will call my college mates and police.

**NITIN**

I am leaving now but I will see you in court. And mind it, it's my apartment not yours.

**MONIKA**

Do whatever you can. I'll face all the challenges but not work with ugly monster like you. Get out at once!

**DISSOLVE TO:**

**INT. MONIKA'S APARTMENT - NEXT DAY**

Monica receives a legal notice from Nitin. She informs her parents and classmates.

**INT. LAWYER'S OFFICE - DAY**

NEHAL's father, a renowned lawyer, takes up Monika's case.

He threatens Nitin on phone.

**NEHAL'S FATHER**

(To Nitin on phone)

Well, Mr Nitin! I have already introduced myself and you know me very well. Monika is my son's colleague and she is not alone now. It would be better if you realise soon and send your written apology as well as the contract signed by Monika. If not , be prepared for police action and newspaper headlines.

**NITIN**

Sorry Sir. No need to go for such drastic steps. It'll spoil my name and fame, Sir. My intent was never bad. I just wanted to help her to have a nice film career. She has got talent and she could be star once her film hits box-office. If she's no more willing to continue, I am ready to break the contract and set her free. I am sending all documents with my written apology, Sir.

**INT. MONIKA'S APARTMENT - DAY**

Monika receives a written apology from Nitin. She moves to hostel and thanks everyone for their support.

She writes a letter to Kalu, explaining everything.

**INT. KALU'S HOUSE - DAY**

Kalu reads Monika's letter, becoming emotional. He writes back, urging her to return to Patna. Monika's reply assures him she will complete her studies first.

**FADE TO BLACK.**

**Note:** Chapter 11 delves into Monika's experiences in the glamorous world of Mumbai's film industry. The screenplay captures her initial excitement, the challenges she faces, and her courage in standing up to unethical behavior.

The chapter also highlights the support she receives from her family, classmates, and a lawyer, reinforcing the theme of community and integrity.

These scenes provide a compelling look at the darker side of fame and success, as well as the strength of character required to navigate such a world.

# Scene 12

**INT. SHARMA RESIDENCE - RANCHI - NIGHT**

Camera opens up panning over Sharma's residence and moves to balcony and over persons sitting there finally focuses on Vinod and Chanda.

VINOD and CHANDA watch their father, MAHANAND SHARMA, enjoying a party with friends, drinking and smoking. CHINTAMANI, their mother, disapproves.

**INT. SHARMA RESIDENCE - KITCHEN - DAY**

Chanda warns Mahanand about Vinod's secret smoking and drinking.

**CHANDA**

(To father Mahanand Sharma)

Papa! Please take care of Vinod. He has started stealing drink from your bottle and makes it up by adding water. Ask him to quit drinking and smoking otherwise he will be spoilt completely.

**SHARMA**

(Laughing)

Oh, that's why my drink getting diluted and I was thinking, the cheater manufacturers making it thinner. Don't worry Chanda like your mum. We are no more orthodox family. For rich ones like us, these happenings are routine. He is preparing to step into his father's shoes.

Mahanand dismisses her concerns, leading to a heated argument.

### INT. SHARMA RESIDENCE - LIVING ROOM - NIGHT

Chintamani and Chanda confront Mahanand about his behavior.

**CHINTAMANI**

(To Mahanand Sharma)

I am warning you. One day you will repent a lot but then it will be too late. Our son is getting spoilt day by day. He doesn't listen to me and grew out of my control. As a father only you can stop him now. He has fallen in bad company.

**SHARMA**

Again same middle class lecture! You are in habbit of spoiling my evening. You filthy drain worms can't tolerate lavish life. My worthy son Vinod only adjusted to this modern life styles and you two fools keep on complaining about him.

**CHANDA**

(Intervening)

Papa! Please listen to mum. She is right. We should return back to our old peaceful life giving up falsehood of lavish life. We will be again a happy lot and there will be no more day to day bickering.

**SHARMA**

(Angrily stands up)

Now, you started teaching your father. Have you grown enough to talk to me like this? This is all because of your mother's support. Rustic fellows!

Mahanand slaps Chanda and storms out.

**CHINTAMANI**

(To Chanda)

He is your father. You should not misbehave with him. I'll handle myself.

### INT. SHARMA RESIDENCE - WORSHIP ROOM - NIGHT

Chintamani and Chanda pray for a solution.

**INT. SHARMA RESIDENCE - LIVING ROOM - DAY**

Chanda overhears Mahanand's phone call about a transfer to Patna. The family celebrates the news.

**INT. KALU'S HOUSE - PATNA - DAY**

Vinod calls Kalu to inform him about the move. Both are excited to reunite.

**INT. SHARMA RESIDENCE - PATNA - DAY**

Mahanand and Chintamani move to Patna. Vinod and Chanda stay in Ranchi for exams.

**EXT. STREET - PATNA - DAY**

Vinod, Chanda, and Kalu enjoy their post-exam holidays. Kalu catches Vinod smoking and lectures him about the dangers of smoking.

**INT. SHARMA RESIDENCE - LIVING ROOM - NIGHT**

Mahanand's health deteriorates. He avoids seeing a doctor until the pain becomes unbearable.

**INT. DOCTOR'S OFFICE - DAY**

The doctor diagnoses Mahanand with liver problems due to alcohol consumption. He warns against further drinking.

**DOCTOR**

(To Mahanand Sharma)

Either you stop drinking or be prepared for heavenly abode.

**SHARMA**

Can I take one peg per day?

**DOCTOR**

For few days only to avoid withdrawal symptoms. But you have to give up alcohol completely in any form.

**SHARMA**

I will, Sir! My family is dearer to me than alcohol. I promise you, Sir. Thanks a lot.

**INT. SHARMA RESIDENCE - LIVING ROOM - NIGHT**

The parties stop, friends drift away, and peace returns to the Sharma household. Kalu convinces Vinod to quit smoking and drinking.

**FADE TO BLACK.**

**Note:** Chapter 12 explores the Sharma family's struggles with Mahanand's indulgence in alcohol and parties, the impact on his children, and the tension it creates within the family.

The screenplay captures the emotional dynamics between family members, the consequences of Mahanand's choices, and the positive transformation that occurs when the family relocates to Patna.

Themes of family values, personal responsibility, and the influence of friends and lifestyle choices are central to this chapter, providing a rich and complex narrative that resonates with broader societal issues.

❑❑

# Scene 13

**INT. KALU'S STUDY ROOM - DAY**

Camera opens up panning over to three students in the room.

Kalu, Vinod, and Chanda are buried in their books, preparing for competitive exams. Tension is palpable.

**INT. KALU'S STUDY ROOM- DAY**

Kalu struggles with stomach pain. His parents are concerned.

**INT. DOCTOR'S OFFICE - DAY**

The doctor diagnoses Kalu with an ulcer in stomach and advises regular meals and less stress alongwith medicines.

**INT. KALU'S STUDY ROOM- NIGHT**

Kalu is torn between studying late and following the doctor's advice.

### INT. GARDEN NEAR BY - DAY

The trio discusses their performances in examinations. Other local friends also gather and boast about their success, shaking confidence of the trio.

**KALU**

(To all)

Let's wait for the results. Hope all of us do well.

### INT. KALU'S LIVING ROOM - DAY

The results of competitions declared. Kalu, Vinod, and Chanda celebrate their success but are saddened by the prospect of separation.

**KALU**

I have got such high rank, that I may get IIT, Delhi.

**CHANDA**

I'll get admission as per my ranking in Patna Medical College itself because of girls getting some domicile preference and it will be convenient for me to study as day scholar. Vinod may opt out of state for better college.

**VINOD**

We all are happy that we have done well. One thing we are missing that we will be separated once again.

**KALU**

Right! But what can be done? We have no choice.

**CHANDA**

One consolation is that we will be together during vacations. Let's vow that we will be spending our vacations at Patna only.

**VINOD & KALU**

Of course. We vow!

**INT. KALU'S BEDROOM - NIGHT**

Kalu reads a letter from Monika. Her face appears against the background of letter speaking aloud

"Hi Kalu! Congratulations for competing in IIT competition. I am also getting admission in law college along with my friend Nehal. Do you remember him? The same guy whose advocate father helped me during my fight with Producer Nitin. He is also a nice guy, always ready to help, just like you. He is tall and handsome and talks sweet. When you come to Mumbai, I will introduce him to you. Any way we will be meeting during summer vacation at Patna".

**KALU**

(feeling a pang of jealousy over her new friendship with Nehal, talks to himself)

Oh! She started liking Nehal. So much nice words about him. It's not her fault. I am black and how can a white beautiful girl like her love me? It's entirely foolish on my part to assume such things.

No, it's may not be so. I am just overthinking. He may be just a colleague. But one thing I must do before it's too late, to write a letter to her expressing my feelings towards her. Yes, I will do it now.

**DISSOLVE TO:**


**INT. KALU'S STUDY ROOM - NIGHT**

Kalu sitting on a chair near study table writes a reply to Monika, then tears it up.

**KALU**

(To himself)

No, it's neither our age nor proper time to get involved in love affair. It's our first duty to concentrate on our study, get a nice job and then do such things like love followed by marriage. What she will think, if she is not in love with me? She may think that I should have seen my ugly black face before proposing love to her. Her high opinion about me will be washed out in a moment.

Now, correct sense has prevailed and I will wait till I get a job with handsome package. Meanwhile further development might help in clearing the murk.

**EXT. PATNA STREET - DAY**

The trio says their goodbyes, promising to stay in touch. Vinod mentions the upcoming mobile phones, but Kalu dismisses the idea as too expensive.

**INT. KALU'S LIVING ROOM - NIGHT**

Kalu packs for Delhi, reflecting on the changes in his life.

**FADE TO BLACK.**

**Note:** Chapter 13 delves into the pressures of competitive exams, the physical toll on Kalu, and the trio's success and impending separation. The chapter also introduces a new emotional dimension to Kalu's relationship with Monika.

The screenplay captures the intensity of their studies, the joy of success, and the bitter-sweet realization that they will be parting ways. It also explores Kalu's internal struggle with his feelings for Monika and his decision to prioritize his studies.

The themes of friendship, ambition, love, and the challenges of growing up continue to be central to the narrative, providing a rich and engaging story that resonates with the experiences of many young people.

# Scene 14

**INT. TRAIN - DAY**

Camera panning over a running train, moving into one compartment and then to Kalu's seat focuses on him.

Kalu, looking out of the window, reflects on leaving home for the first time. He's filled with regret and sadness.

**INT. SAME COMPARTMENT OF TRAIN - NIGHT**

Kalu struggles to eat and sleep, feeling the weight of his loneliness. But any how remembering his mother's instructions of regular eating and sleeping, he opens the lunch box and takes few bites. After gulping water from the bottle he asks newspaper from the uncle sitting in front of him. In no time, he falls asleep while reading newspaper.

**EXT. NEW DELHI STATION – DAY**

Kalu arrives in Delhi, feeling overwhelmed by the unknown city. He takes an auto to reach hostel.

**INT. HOSTEL ROOM - DAY**

Kalu meets his roommates, ALOK MOHAPATRA from Odisha and VIJAY MAHADEVAN from Tamil Nadu. Language barriers create initial awkwardness.

**INT. HOSTEL ROOM - NIGHT**

Mahapatra falls ill. Mahadevan provides medicines taking advice from his doctor father. Kalu helps Mahadevan communicate with the mess worker, LALIT, to get food packed in tiffin for Mahapatra. The bond between roommates gets stronger with this incident and they start sharing experiences without any hesitation.

**INT. CLASSROOMS/HOSTEL - MONTAGE**

The roommates come closer, learning each other's languages and cultures. Kalu struggles academically but finds support from his roommates.

**INT. HOSTEL ROOM - NIGHT**

Kalu's health deteriorates due to stress of late night study. At one time he thinks of dropping his study midway as he used to miss morning classes because of rising late and as a result of it he was getting lower grades in exam.

Mahadevan finding him anxious decides to talk to him.

**MAHADEVAN**

(To Kalu)

Why are you looking so ill and exhausted? I am not finding you in the morning classes regularly. Is everything ok?

**MAHAPATRA**

No dear, he is not well. I myself
wanted to talk to you regarding
this. He is in both mental and
physical stress and needs our help.
I will help him in his study if he
doesn't mind and you ask your father
and provide him some medicines.

### KALU

Thanks both of you. I really need
your help otherwise I will have to
drop the course midway.

### MAHADEVAN

You should have told us before. Now
we are bosom friends and we will
have to solve our problems by
sharing with each other. Don't
worry! I and Mahapatra will do
whatever needed and you will see the
results within a fortnight.

### MAHAPATRA

Stop late night study. Sleep early
and rise early. Take regular meals
including morning breakfast. Ask

frankly wherever you need help in study. Every thing will be fine.

With help from Mahapatra and Mahadevan, Kalu finds right balance and improves his grades too alongwith improvement in health.

### INT. CLASSROOM - DAY

Mohapatra bursts in, alerting the class about a fight involving few outsiders and a classmate, PINAKI.

### EXT. COLLEGE CAMPUS - DAY

Students rush to the scene, some armed with hockey sticks and cricket bats. They catch hold of three of them and rest outsiders run away seeing the coming mob of students. As students are beating the outsiders, Kalika and Mahadevan soon realise that any death may worsen the situation. So with help of few other right thinking colleagues stop the fight and call the police.

**INT. PRINCIPAL'S OFFICE- DAY**

The principal intervenes, trying to keep the incident under carpet. But students not succumbing to pressure, insist with the police to raid and arrest the culprits. Later police uncovers a drug ring within 24hrs, leading to arrests of kingpins. With de-addiction treatments of few drug taking students, the drug menace ends completely in the campus.

**FADE TO BLACK.**

**Note:** Chapter 14 follows Kalu's journey to Delhi, his struggles with loneliness, and his eventual bonding with his roommates. The chapter also explores the challenges of academic life and the unexpected incident involving drugs in campus.

The screenplay captures Kalu's emotional journey, from his initial regret and sadness to his growing connection with his roommates and his determination to succeed academically. The incident with the drug ring adds an element of drama and highlights the importance of community and solidarity among the students.

The themes of friendship, personal growth, cultural understanding, and the challenges of young adulthood continue to be central to the narrative, providing a rich and engaging story.

❑❑

## Scene 15

**INT. ANATOMY DEPARTMENT - PATNA MEDICAL COLLEGE - DAY**

Camera opens up panning over few students entering dissection hall, through to dead bodies lying there and then focuses on Chanda's face.

Chanda enters, her face contorted with discomfort from the smell of formalin. She's surrounded by fellow students, including KHUSHBU and SHYAMAL.

**CHANDA:** (to herself) I can't tolerate this smell and look of dead body and we have to sit by its side.

**KHUSHBU:**

(grinning)

Not just sitting beside it, the dead body has to be dissected by us. Make it habbit, slowly you will get used to it and everything will be easy.

**CHANDA:**

(surprised)

How did you know what I was thinking?

**SHYAMAL:**

(teasing)

Why not? When you've tolerated the living ghosts, this dead man won't even tease you.

Chanda smiles slightly, a rare occurrence.

**INT. HOSTEL BATHROOM - DAY**

Chanda scrubs herself, trying to get rid of the smell of formalin.

**INT. VINOD'S HOSTEL ROOM - CALCUTTA - NIGHT**

VINOD is on the phone with Chanda, laughing and sharing stories.

**VINOD:**

Today we all had to get our blood drawn from each other.

**CHANDA:**

(curious)

Now blood will also have to be given, but why?

**VINOD:**

(laughing)

You crazy girl, we study how to test blood in practicals. Will we draw the blood of a dog?

**CHANDA**

(To herself)

Now, I have a solution to this problem. I will make Shyamal, sacrificing goat.

**INT. PATNA MEDICAL COLLEGE- DAY**

Chanda's relationship with Shyamal grows, and her friends tease her.

**POONAM:** (pulling Chanda's ear) Wow, great. You trapped a lover or bonded labourer?

**DIVYA:** (playfully) Ek bandhua pal liya hai ! ek banda pal liya hai...

Chanda laughs and retorts, enjoying the banter.

**INT. VINOD'S HOSTEL - CALCUTTA - DAY**

Thefts are happening daily. MADAN discovers his transistor missing.

**MADAN:** (frantic) My transistor is gone!

They search the rooms, find evidence against AMAN, and call the police.

**WARDEN:** (serious) We'll have to expel him.

### INT. HOSTEL - CALCUTTA - LATER

The boys of the hostel sigh in relief, the thief caught and expelled.

### FADE TO BLACK.

**Note:** This chapter delves into the daily lives of Chanda and Vinod, exploring their experiences in medical college and the relationships they form. Chanda's interactions with Shyamal and her friends add depth to her character, showing her ability to adapt and find joy in her challenging environment. Vinod's experience with the theft in his hostel adds a layer of intrigue and highlights the complexities of communal living.

The screenplay captures the humor, challenges, and camaraderie that define their experiences, setting the stage for further development in the characters and their relationships.

❑❑

# Scene 16

**EXT. PATNA - DAY - SUMMER VACATION**

Camera opens capturing Sun in sky and back to garden and focuses over a gathering of students

The hot sun beats down on the city. Friends and groups are gathered, celebrating the joy of passing the first year of higher education.

**INT. MONIKA'S HOUSE - DAY**

MONIKA, CHANDA, KALIKA, and VINOD are gathered, sharing stories and laughter. Monika's fashion-forward appearance and newfound debating skills are evident.

**MONIKA:** (to Kalika) I've become quite the debater, haven't I?

**KALIKA:** (grinning) Law school does that to you.

**CHANDA:** (teasing) And Monika, Mumbai's fashion world has changed you completely!

They laugh, share mangoes, litchis, samosas, and rasgullas, enjoying each other's company.

**EXT. PARK - EVENING**

Monika and Kalu sit on a bench, catching up.

**MONIKA:** (serious) You've changed, Kalu. You've become distant.

**KALU:** (defensively) You've changed too. Mumbaikars don't like to be touched by small-town boys, do they?

**MONIKA:** (softly) You'll always be my best friend, Kalu, no matter you become delhite or remain Patnaite.

They talk late into the night, clearing misunderstandings.

**EXT. PARK - NEXT EVENING**

Monika hands Kalu a mobile phone.

**MONIKA:** Now we can keep in touch all the time.

**KALU:** (hesitant) But it's so expensive...

**VINOD:** (arriving with Chanda) It's common now. Chanda and I have one too.

They gossip and enjoy their time together.

**EXT. PATNA - DAYS/NIGHTS**

The holidays fly by, filled with joy, anxiety, and unspoken feelings.

Kalu struggles with his love for Monika but never finds the courage to confess.

**EXT. PATNA RAILWAY STATION - DAY**

Chanda drops Kalu at the station, teasing him about his unspoken love.

**CHANDA:** (whispering) Don't delay in telling the matters of the heart, Kalu.

**KALU:** (nervous) It's not like that...

The train blows whistle, and Chanda sends Kalu off with a smile.

**FADE TO BLACK.**

**Note:** Chapter 16 is filled with the warmth of friendship, the joy of reuniting, and the unspoken feelings that linger between friends. The introduction of mobile phones symbolizes a new era and the growing connection between the characters, even as they part ways.

The screenplay captures the essence of youthful exuberance, the excitement of new experiences, and the bitter-sweet nature of growing up and moving apart. The underlying emotions, especially Kalu's unspoken love for Monika, add depth and complexity to the relationships, setting the stage for future developments.

❏❏

## Scene 17

### INT. HOSTEL - DAY

Camera opens up panning over hostel and focuses on students gathered there.

Students are bustling around, organizing new rooms and adjusting to new roommates. VINOD is excitedly capturing the first image of his doctor's profile with stethoscope around his neck on his mobile camera.

### INT. HOSPITAL - DAY

VINOD is examining a patient, noting down details. He presents his findings to the DOCTOR TEACHER, who praises him.

**DOCTOR TEACHER:** Good, very good, Vinod.

VINOD shares his achievement with his family and friends, receiving congratulations and a similar photo from CHANDA.

#### INT. COLLEGE - DAY

VINOD and classmates are caught attempting to introduce themselves to fresh first-year students. They are brought before the disciplinary committee.

**HEAD OF ANATOMY:** (stern) This is unacceptable behavior.

They are suspended but later reinstated with a warning. VINOD becomes introverted and serious.

#### INT. HOSTEL - NIGHT

VINOD's friends notice his changed behavior and inform the WARDEN, DR. DIWAKAR.

**DR. DIWAKAR:** (concerned) We need to help him.

VINOD is taken to psychiatrist DR. TONDON and improves after attending regular counseling.sessions.

**EXT. HOSPITAL - DAY**

CHANDA is attracted to PRATYUSH, a postgraduate student in the Department of Medicine. They spend time together in the ward, by the Ganges, and in the canteen.

**INT. WOMEN'S HOSTEL - EVENING**

CHANDA and PRATYUSH chat in the courtyard. Their relationship becomes talk of the campus as an established pair at Patna Medical College.

**ONE GIRL:** (seeing Chanda coming) At least competition for one seat lessened in PG course admission in Gynaecology department. Now, Chanda is interested more in medicine.

**ANOTHER GIRL:** Who knows? She might stick to Gynaecology, brother may opt for anesthesia, bhabhi paediatric and Pratyush already in medicine. Then, comfortably plan for running Nursing home or maybe a big hospital.

**THIRD GIRL:** Don't be jealous. Search your own pet, please.

The whole group start laughing. In stead of getting irritated, Chanda throws back flying kiss to them with glittering smile.

### INT. CHANDA'S HOME - NIGHT

CHANDA convinces her parents to allow her to stay in the hostel.

**CHANDA:** Group study is more effective, Papa. Because of evening classes in the ward I am already returning late in the evening. So, better I reside in the hostel.

**FATHER:** I know you better. These are filmsy excuses to remain away from the family and enjoy freedom. Many have become well qualified doctors studying at home.

**CHANDA:** Mummy, please. If Papa will remain admant, I will go on indefinite fast.

After a hunger strike, her father agrees, and she is allotted a room.

**EXT. DESERTED PLACES - VARIOUS TIMES**

CHANDA and PRATYUSH meet secretly, fearing the word reaching their families. They take occasional help from friends, sharing romantic stories of their meetings.

**FADE TO BLACK.**

**Note:** Chapter 17 explores the growth and changes in the characters. VINOD's journey from excitement to introspection after a disciplinary incident shows his maturation. His counseling experience adds depth to his character, showing his vulnerability and resilience.

CHANDA's blossoming romance with PRATYUSH adds a new dimension to the story. Their relationship, filled with secret meetings and shared dreams, captures the excitement and fear of young love.

The chapter also highlights the influence of technology, with mobile phones playing a significant role in communication and self-expression.

The screenplay treatment captures these themes, providing a rich and engaging continuation of the characters' journeys.

❑❑

# Scene 18

### INT. KALIKA'S ROOM - DAY

Camera panning over hostel, moves inside towards Kalu's room and focuses on Kalu with broom in his hand.

KALIKA PRASAD (KALU) is cleaning his room when he notices the mobile phone. He hesitates, then dials MONIKA'S number.

### INT. MONIKA'S ROOM - DAY

MONIKA answers, teasing KALU for not calling earlier. They chat, but KALU's doubts prevent him from expressing his feelings.

### EXT. COLLEGE CAMPUS - DAY

KALU is walking to class when PRIYA, a classmate, approaches him.

**PRIYA:** Kalika! Alone today? Where are the others?

**KALU:** (witty) If they were together, where would I have got this opportunity to talk to you?

They chat briefly, and PRIYA invites KALU to meet her at the hostel sometime.

### EXT. CAFETERIA - DAY

PRIYA bumps into KALU again and convinces him to have tea with her. They find a corner table and chat, with KALU slowly becoming more comfortable.

**PRIYA:** (playful) I wanted to say something to you many times, but hesitated because of your introverted nature.

**KALU:** I have to hurry up today because of some prefixed assignment. Better next time.

They part ways, promising to meet again.

### EXT. CAMPUS - DAY

PRIYA meets MANPREET KAUR, revealing a bet they have made about KALU. They laugh and agree on new terms.

**MANPREET:** I tell you again. He is not like other guys who run after the girl.

**PRIYA:** If you are so confident, double the amount of bet. You will see him waiting for me at the gate of girls' hostel.

**MANPREET:** You try your best. I give you two weeks time.

**PRIYA:** done!

### INT. KALU'S ROOM - NIGHT

KALU is restless, thinking about PRIYA's behavior. He calls CHANDA and tells her everything.

**CHANDA:** (advising) Be a little careful with them. There is nothing wrong with light interaction. Just be smart and don't be fooled.

KALU falls asleep, comforted by CHANDA's advice.

**EXT. COLLEGE CAMPUS - VARIOUS DAYS**

PRIYA continues to ambush KALU, inviting him to the hostel. KALU avoids giving assurance. PRIYA eventually accepts defeat and pays MANPREET the bet money, regretting her behavior.

**FADE TO BLACK**

**Note:** Chapter 18 delves into the complexities of friendship, doubt, and the games people play. KALU's internal struggle between his heart and mind, his hesitation to express his feelings to MONIKA, and his interactions with PRIYA all add layers to his character.

PRIYA's bet with MANPREET and her attempts to win KALU over provide a humorous subplot that also serves to highlight the differences in character and behavior among the students.

The chapter also emphasizes the importance of trust and genuine connection, as seen in KALU's conversation with CHANDA and his refusal to be swayed by PRIYA's superficial advances.

The screenplay treatment captures these themes, weaving them into a narrative that continues to explore the characters' growth and the dynamics of their relationships.

❑❑

## Scene 19

**EXT. COLLEGE CAMPUS - DAY**

Camera panning over the road moves on to different groups of students loitering and focuses on to Nehal.

NEHAL tries to call MONIKA, but she doesn't respond. He's confused and worried.

**INT. CANTEEN - DAY**

NEHAL's friends discuss MONIKA's absence and tease NIRBHAY about his feelings for her. They all stop talking as NEHAL joins them, lost in thought.

**INT. NEHAL'S ROOM - NIGHT**

NEHAL struggles with sleep, tormented by thoughts of MONIKA and what might have happened. He reflects on their relationship and fears the worst.

**EXT. COLLEGE CAMPUS - DAY (10 DAYS LATER)**

NEHAL is in a daze, consumed by loneliness and uncertainty. He prays for Monika's return and a chance to express his feelings.

**EXT. COLLEGE CAMPUS - DAY (15 DAYS LATER)**

MONIKA surprises NEHAL, slapping him playfully from behind.

**MONIKA:** What's the matter? In whose remembrance are you slowly moving forward without even knowing about the world?

**NEHAL:** (forcing a smile) Nothing, just the exam is coming closer, worrying about it.

**MONIKA** (revealing) I have been away for my sudden engagement and my wedding is scheduled next month. You will have to attend it .

NEHAL is devastated but hides his emotions.

**NEHAL:** Of course, not attending your wedding, it can't happen. You are my closest friend and nothing matters more to me than your happiness.

They agree to have a party with friends on Saturday.

NEHAL rushes back to his hostel with broken heart, stopping tears coming out of his eyes with great effort.

### INT. NEHAL'S ROOM – DAY (LATER)

NEHAL is alone, overwhelmed by grief. He allows himself to cry, his dreams shattered.

### FADE TO BLACK

**Note:** Chapter 19 is a poignant and emotional turning point in the story. NEHAL's unspoken love for MONIKA is brought to the forefront, only to be crushed by the revelation of her engagement and upcoming wedding.

The screenplay treatment captures the tension, uncertainty, and heartbreak that NEHAL experiences. His internal struggle is portrayed through his interactions with friends, his restless nights, and his desperate prayers for a chance to express his feelings.

MONIKA'S return and the casual way she shares the news of her engagement add to the tragedy of the situation. NEHAL's efforts to hide his true emotions and his promise to celebrate her happiness, despite his own pain, underscore the depth of his feelings and the complexity of their relationship.

The chapter ends on a note of profound sadness, setting the stage for further developments in the characters' lives and relationships.

# Scene 20

### INT. TECHNICAL FAIR VENUE - DAY

Camera opens up panning over preparation going on for technical fair and focuses on Kalu.

KALIKA PRASAD is busy with preparations for the technical fair. He's excited to share his achievements with friends.

### INT. CANTEEN - DAY

KALIKA's phone rings. It's CHANDA, sounding nervous. He eats quickly and calls her back, but she's busy. A black cat crosses his path, and he feels a bad omen.

### EXT. COLLEGE CAMPUS - DAY

KALIKA walking towards hostel

MONIKA calls KALIKA, announcing her engagement and upcoming wedding.

KALIKA is speechless, heartbroken but congratulates her.

### INT. KALIKA'S ROOM - DAY

KALIKA stares at himself in the mirror, feeling dark and unworthy.

**KALIKA:** (talking to himself) How dare you fool! Your own mother hates your black complexion and you dreaming of a white angel Monika as your life partner. It's height of Idiocy.

Suddenly Mobile rings and the very ringtone infuriates him.

**KALIKA:** (about to throw mobile angrily) Why are you ringing now. This costly gift from her added fuel to my misunderstood love fire.

(Stops midway) Oh! It's Chanda, the best friend of mine.

(Picks up phone) I know Chanda what bad news you want to share with me.

**CHANDA:** Take care of yourself. It happens in our life. We girls can't express our wish and so is the case of Monika. Though you two never shared your feelings with each other but even if you have done that the result would have been the same. Monika and you would have never gone against the wishes of your middle class family where love marriage is almost forebidden. Take my case. I am in love with Pratyush but neither he nor I have still informed our family. We are sitting on a ticking dynamite as we can't imagine life without eachother.

**KALIKA:** Don't worry, Chanda! Your friend Kalu will solve it out. If you allow, I may talk to Vinod and we two will make others ready for your marriage.

**CHANDA:** I know it. But just wait. First of all, let Pratyush talk with his parents and then we'll go accordingly.

**KALIKA:** (forgetting own pain) Yes, you sound more genuine. Keep me informed time to time and everything will be ok. Bye!

**CHANDA:** Bye, take care!

**INT. TECHNICAL FAIR VENUE - DAY (FOUR DAYS LATER)**

KALIKA receives honor for his work in the technical fair. His wound starts to heal.

**EXT. COLLEGE CAMPUS - DAY**

KALIKA's phone rings. It's NEHAL, Monika's classmate from Mumbai. They discuss Monika's marriage and extend a hand of friendship to each other.

**NEHAL:** Today evening in the college canteen there is a party of classmates to celebrate her marriage being fixed. It is known that the boy is running a big business in London and his parents have two-three petrol pumps in Kanpur. They are high profile family. Monika is very lucky to have such hubby.

**KALIKA:** Yes, indeed. We all want her to remain happy always. Ok, now I will have to go for meal. Mess time is about to end. Will call you later.

**NEHAL:** OK, we will remain good friends in future. Please keep myself in touch.

They hang up, promising to continue talking in the future.

**FADE TO BLACK**

**Note:** Chapter 20 explores the complex emotions surrounding love, friendship, and heartbreak. KALIKA's reaction to Monika's engagement is a central focus, and his conversations with CHANDA and NEHAL provide insight into the different ways people cope with unrequited love and societal pressures.

The screenplay treatment captures the emotional journey of the characters, from KALIKA's initial excitement about the technical fair to his devastation at Monika's news, his support for CHANDA, and his unexpected connection with NEHAL.

The chapter also touches on themes of fate, self-worth, and the human tendency to find solace in shared pain. The black cat crossing KALIKA's path symbolizes his sense of foreboding, while his reflection in the mirror represents his struggle with self-acceptance.

The interactions between the characters are rich with subtext, and the dialogue conveys their complex emotions and relationships. The chapter ends on a note of tentative hope and connection, setting the stage for further developments in the story.

❏❏

## Scene 21

**INT. WEDDING VENUE - DAY**

Camera panning from decorated welcome gate moving to cover decorated house .

The melodious sound of shehnai fills the air. Guests arrive, and preparations are underway for the reception of the barat next day evening. CHANDA and BINDU, Kalu's elder sister, are among those planning to tease the groom. NEERAJ, Kalu's elder brother, and other boys including KALIKA( Kalu), VINOD, and NEHAL are busy arranging beds and other facilities of staying place for the baraat when it will reach tomorrow afternoon.

**INT. KITCHEN - DAY**

Confectioners are busy preparing snacks and sweets. On the other side cooks are preparing lunch and dinner for today.. MONIKA'S maternal uncle oversees the store of the kitchen. The boys of the locality handle the responsibility of serving the food to guests.

### INT. MANDAP - NIGHT

The ceremony of applying turmeric to MONIKA begins. Family members one by one coming towards Monika, applying turmeric and blessing her. Women are seen singing folk songs related to marriage and joking.

**SOME LADY:**

Look the face of bride shining like moon. When the groom will lift the veil, he will lose all his senses. He will forget english women forever.

Every one agrees with her observation, Monka blushing with shame.


Uncle applies turmeric paste on Monika's mother's face. This signals starting of mad race with males and females running after each other to apply turmeric paste.

The atmosphere is lively, and everyone eventually proceeds to the pandal for dinner.

### EXT. WEDDING VENUE - DAY (NEXT DAY)

Decorators, flower vendors, and others are busy with preparations. MONIKA is anxious to meet KALU and asks CHANDA to bring him to her.

### INT. COURTYARD - DAY

CHANDA finds KALU and brings him to MONIKA. They have a heartfelt conversation, where MONIKA confesses her love for KALU and he acknowledges his feelings for her.

**MONIKA:** I loved you a lot since childhood, but I felt that I didn't know, what did you think. In this confusion, I could never say anything. I must have seen something in your eyes many times, but how could I have complete faith, unless you expressed yourself. Atleast you should have given sufficient hints. Even today you are hiding your feelings though I can read vividly in your eyes. It is very hard in our society for a girl to confess her love unless she is sure that he loves her too. Otherwise she is branded as cheap. Had it been other way round and I would have been a boy and you girl, it would have been better. I am expressing it today because it will not make any difference now and I don't want to carry the guilt in my mind that I never told you.

**KALU:** Khuda Hafiz! If life ever gives me another chance, I will try to act with courage. May you live happily forever with your life-partner, this is my prayer from the bottom of my heart.

**MONIKA:** Now forget me. Marry a charming girl. I wish to see you with one son sitting on your left shoulder and one daughter holding your right hand with a bag filled with vegetables in your left hand.

**KALU:** Can't promise but will try to fulfill your wish. Good Bye. I'll not say 'Alvida' as our friendship will continue till death.

They part with tears in their eyes, and CHANDA observes the exchange.

### EXT. COMMUNITY HALL - NIGHT

The barat procession leaves for the bride's house, with music, lights, and dancing. The bride and her friends watch from the terrace.

### INT. WEDDING VENUE - NIGHT

The groom is pulled from the car to dance. The exchange of garlands takes place, and the baraatis are invited to eat. The marriage is solemnized after midnight.

**FADE TO BLACK**

**Note:** Chapter 21 is a poignant and emotional chapter that centers around the wedding of MONIKA. The preparations, ceremonies, and festivities are described in vivid detail, creating a lively and colorful backdrop for the story.

The heart of the chapter lies in the private conversation between MONIKA and KALU, where they acknowledge their unspoken love for each other. This moment is filled with regret, longing, and a sense of what might have been. Their farewell is bittersweet, and the emotions are palpable.

The chapter also introduces new characters and relationships, adding depth to the world of the story. The interactions between family and friends are warm and authentic, capturing the spirit of a traditional Indian wedding.

The screenplay treatment highlights the key events and emotional beats of the chapter, translating the rich narrative into a visual and dramatic format. The wedding provides a vibrant setting, and the unspoken love between MONIKA and KALU adds a layer of complexity and emotion to the story.

❏❏

# Scene 22

**INT. COLLEGE CAMPUS - DAY**

Camera opens up panning the waiting hall focuses on to Kalu sitting on a chair.

KALU, dressed in formal attire, is among a group of students waiting for their turn for the interview. The atmosphere is tense. He takes a deep breath and enters the interview room.

**INT. INTERVIEW ROOM - DAY**

KALU faces a panel of interviewers from a prestigious foreign company. He answers their questions confidently, impressing them.

**INT. COLLEGE CAMPUS - LATER**

KALU exits the interview room, looking hopeful as he has cleared first two rounds and is to appear next rounds tomorrow. He meets his friends, MOHAPATRA and MAHADEVAN, who are disappointed with their results. MAHADEVAN shares tips with KALU for the next rounds.

**INT. INTERVIEW ROOM- NEXT DAY (EVENING)**

KALU is in the last round which they call HR round.

**HR MANAGER:**

I am glad to announce that you are selected for the job in our Company.

Now, what is your expectations regarding salary and other benefits.

**KALU:** I am expecting around 30 lacs gross salary with handsome equity shares and other benefits company provides to its employees.

**HR MANAGER**

You are smart guy having accurate estimation of your worth. Agreed with your proposal. Soon, we will finish all the formalities and send your appointment letter by email. Congratulations.

**KALU**

Thanks Sir!


Tears of joy start rolling down his face, as he comes out. News spreads like wildfire, and he is surrounded by classmates, celebrating his success.

**INT. HOSTEL ROOM - NIGHT**


KALU calls his family to share the good news. He hears the pride in their voices, especially his mother's. VINOD and CHANDA also congratulate him.

**INT. COLLEGE CAMPUS - NEXT DAY**

KALU distributes sweets to teachers and students. He becomes a campus celebrity overnight, with juniors looking up to him.

**INT. HOSTEL ROOM - NIGHT**

KALU receives a call from MONIKA, who is now in Mumbai with her husband VIKRAM. They congratulate him and discuss Monika's decision to continue her studies. KALU advises patience to VIKRAM and persuades him to allow her to do so.

**INT. COLLEGE LIBRARY - DAY**

As exam dates approach, KALU is engrossed in his studies. MAHADEVAN and MOHAPATRA support him, reminding him not to take stress too much as he has nothing to prove now.

**INT. COLLEGE CAFETERIA - DAY**

The three friends discuss their future plans. While MOHAPATRA considers higher studies or the Indian Administrative Service, KALU and MAHADEVAN decide to work for a few years before pursuing master's degrees.

**FADE TO BLACK**

**Note:** Chapter 22 delves into the pressures and joys of college life, especially during the crucial placement season. KALU's unexpected success and the subsequent celebrations highlight the roller-coaster of emotions students have to go through. The chapter also touches upon the importance of friendship and support during trying times. The screenplay treatment captures these key moments and emotions, providing a visual narrative of the chapter's events.

# Scene 23

**INT. HYDERABAD AIRPORT - DAY (AFTER 10 YEARS)**

Camera panning from outside airport moving into boarding gate focuses on Kalu and his family.

KALU, his wife SUNANDA, and their children SHREYA and PULKIT are waiting for their flight to Patna. The mood is somber as they've just learned of Kalu's mother's death.

**INT. AIRPLANE - DAY**

The family is in their seats, lost in thought. SUNANDA reflects on her complicated relationship with her mother-in-law. KALU is choked with emotion but tries to remain strong for his children.

**EXT. PATNA - KALU'S FAMILY HOME - DAY**

The family arrives at the house, filled with mourners.

**SHREYA:** Mummy ! Why so many people gathered here at our grand father's house.

CAMERA shifts and focuses on to a dead body lying in lobby. ZOOMING over the face of dead body just opened by BINDU, then focuses back on to SHREYA.

**SHREYA:** (weeping) Papa! Grand Maa is no more. She left us for heavenly abode.

PULKIT, KALU and SUNANDA also breaks down. The family and neighbours joins in the grief.

**EXT. BANKS OF THE GANGES - DAY**

The men of the family, led by KALU's father DAYA PRASAD, prepare for the cremation. A debate ensues over traditional vs. electric cremation, and NEERAJ, Kalu's brother, settles the matter in favour of electric cremation.

**EXT. DHABA - DAY**

After the cremation, the family gathers at a local eatery to satiate hunger as per custom. The mood shifts as they return to normalcy.

**KALU:** (to himself)

How transient is nature of life or death! How short is the period of cremation salvation! People discussing of falsehood of illusion in daily life just few minutes ago, are now busy in relishing puri and jalebi and saying that rasgulla and gulab jamun would have been better.

**INT. KALU'S FAMILY HOME - EVENING**

The family discusses the upcoming rituals and decides to follow traditional practices for thirteen days. DAYA PRASAD takes charge of the arrangements. All brothers contribute money for expenses of rituals and Daya Babu hands it over to his eldest son Neeraj.

**INT. KALU'S FAMILY HOME - NIGHT**

KALU, alone in a secluded corner, sobs quietly. He hears his father crying in the bathroom and realizes the depth of his loss. He contemplates inviting his father to live with him in Hyderabad.

**FADE TO BLACK**

**Note:** Chapter 23 explores the complex emotions surrounding the death of a family member. It delves into the rituals, debates, and dynamics that unfold in the wake of a loss. The chapter also highlights the intricate relationships within the family, including the bond between a mother-in-law and daughter-in-law, the expectations placed on men to remain stoic, and the realization of a void left by a loved one's passing away.

The screenplay treatment captures these themes by focusing on key scenes and interactions. It provides a visual narrative that conveys the emotional journey of the characters as they navigate grief, tradition, and the inevitable return to daily life.

❏❏

# Scene 24

**INT. KALU'S FAMILY HOME - MORNING**

Camera panning from outside of the house moves in and around.

The house is filled with the hustle and bustle of preparations for the twelfth-day rituals after the death of KALU's mother. The mood is somber but purposeful. Family members are busy with various tasks.

**EXT. KALU'S FAMILY HOME - LATE AFTERNOON**

Guests arrive, including VINOD, CHANDA, and their families. KALU and SUNANDA greet them warmly. Their children alongwith SHREYA and PULKIT, play together, forming a bond after being introduced to each other and sent off to play.

**INT. KALU'S FAMILY HOME - DINING AREA - NIGHT**

The group sits around a table, enjoying dinner and conversation. VINOD shares his recent visit to London and meeting with MONIKA and her son MAKALU. KALU's phone rings, and he steps away to take the call from MONIKA. They share a brief, emotional conversation about the loss. KALU returns to the table, visibly moved.

**EXT. KALU'S FAMILY HOME - NIGHT**

NEHAL, a lawyer and another old friend, arrives. KALU greets him with joy and surprise. The group reminisces about the past, their college days, and Monika's wedding. NEHAL shares his decision to remain unmarried and his growing interest in politics. The conversation is filled with nostalgia, laughter, and some bitter-sweet moments.

**INT. KALU'S FAMILY HOME - MORNING - NEXT DAY**

The family prepares for the worship of Lord Satyanarayana. There's a sense of closure and acceptance. NEERAJ, KALU's brother, reflects on the rituals and how these have helped the family cope with the unbearable loss. The rituals are performed with reverence and solemnity.

**EXT. KALU'S FAMILY HOME - EVENING**

Guests start to leave. DAYA BABU, KALU's father, is adamant about staying in the family home alongwith the memories of his late wife. The family arranges for help to take care of him. Emotional farewells are exchanged.

**INT. KALU'S FAMILY HOME - DAYA BABU'S ROOM - NIGHT**

DAYA BABU struggles with loneliness. He spends his nights reading or meditating, trying to find solace in the memories of his late wife. Close-ups of his face reveal his pain and longing. The room is filled with mementos and photographs of his late wife.

**FADE TO BLACK**

**Note:** Chapter 24 delves deep into the healing process after a significant loss. It showcases the importance of rituals, the support of friends and family, and the challenges of coping with grief. The chapter also touches upon the complexities of relationships, the passage of time, and the inevitability of moving on.

The screenplay treatment captures the essence of the chapter by focusing on key interactions and emotional moments. It provides a visual narrative that portrays the journey of the characters as they navigate through their grief, find support in each other, and gradually come to terms with their loss.

❏❏

# Scene 25

**INT. KALU AND SUNANDA'S BEDROOM - MORNING**

Camera panning. Kalu's house from outside moves into bedroom focuses on to Sunanda.

SUNANDA, emotional, sits on the bed. KALU is getting ready for work.

**SUNANDA:** We have closeness, affection, familiarity, but something seems missing. This husband-wife relationship of ours is sweet, but I can't call it love. You will also agree, atleast both of us don't believe in show off. That's why, we don't greet each other with false love messages as some pairs do.

**KALU:** (Defensively) If there's any lack of honesty in our relationship, tell me. Have I ever neglected you? If everything is going well, what's the point of this useless puzzle?

He leaves the room, unsettled.

**INT. KALU'S OFFICE - DAY**

KALU sits at his desk, sipping tea, reflecting.

**KALU:** (to himself) Sunanda was not uttering useless things in the morning. She was right that love is not at all essential in leading successful married life because it needs a balancing act through compromises on either side. Rather it is sense of responsibility which is required more, while in love an iota of irresponsiblity and arrogance creepps in though in the name of freedom. Something you can't share with your spouse though you easily share it with your friends. The absence of love in our relationship may be because of my unsuccessful first love with Monika.

Phone RINGS. It's MONIKA.

**KALU**: (to himself before picking up the phone) It's true when you remember some one, he/she may be present that very moment

**MONIKA**: How are you? Three months have passed waiting for your call. Sir, didn't you get time at all?"

**KALU**: Yes, was about to do it. A little depression had taken over after the passing of my mother. How are you guys doing? Are you practicing law at London?

**MONIKA**: We are fine here but we have shifted to Los Angeles in California state of America because of transfer of Vikram's business head office to this place. As my son Makalu is too young, he needs me for his day to day care, so I remain busy. I will practice law after two to three years. How about you? Got married or still single?

**KALU**: Yeah! I am married to Sunanda and have one daughter Shreya and one son Pulkit as you wished at the time of your marriage with Vikram. They all are doing well.

They catch up, discuss their lives, families, and careers.

**MONIKA:** I will meet you all whenever I come to India and I will call you every now and then. You just give me a miss-call whenever you want to talk.

**KALU:** I will. Take care.

He hangs up, sensing something might be wrong but dismisses it.

**INT. KALU AND SUNANDA'S HOME - EVENING**

KALU returns home. SUNANDA behaves normally. They talk to DAYA BABU on the phone.

**SUNANANDA:** Pranam Papa! How are you? We are fine. Shreya and Pulkit always remember you and asks me to invite you here to live with us, if not permanently, atleast for a month or so.

**DAYA BABU:** Remain happy, you all. Bindu has come with her children for 15 days. Neeraj will be coming here after two months. I am getting opportunity to enjoy with my grandchildren.

**KALU:** After their departure, you come to Hyderabad and spend a few months with us. Shreya and Pulkit should also get your affection and blessings.

**DAYA BABU:** (Noncommittal) I see.

They plan a visit to Patna in December.

**INT. DAYA BABU'S BEDROOM - NIGHT**

DAYA BABU's grandchildren, PRADYUMAN and AARADHYA, burst into his room.

**PRADYUMAN & AARADHYA:** Grandfather, Grandfather! Tell us a story!

**DAYA BABU:** I can't tell a story as good as your grandmother used to, but I'll try.

**PRADYUMAN & AARADHYA:** Okay! But it should be of King, Queen and Prince

He tells them a fairy tale that subtly mirrors his own life with his late wife.

**DAYA BABU:** (To grandchildren on either side) A lovely Prince Aditya was born to King Vishisht and Queen Sukhmayi. When Aditya grew into handsome youth, he saw a beautiful princess Padmavati in a temple of some other kingdom where he wandered while hunting. On his insistence, he was married to Padmavati. Later on her instigation, he attacked a neighbouring Kingdom and grabbing the throne, settled there leaving parents behind.

In truth, Padmavati was a magician and one day she lost to the greatest magician of world and had to shift to his magical palace.

Daya Babu gives a look towards children who are yawning.

**DAYA BABU:** (Softly) As soon as this happened, all his magic also ended. The palace alongwith entire Kingdom vanished and the prince found himself in a deserted wilderness, from where there was no way to come out.

The children fall asleep, leaving DAYA BABU lost in thought and loneliness.

**DAYA BABU:** (To himself) Even though the world may name conjugal love to

Nayantara ji's witchcraft magic, but today he is cursed to live in the wilderness of loneliness that she's left behind for the rest of his life.


**FADE TO BLACK.**


**Themes and Notes:**


This screenplay maintains the themes of love, relationships, and loneliness from the chapter. The dialogues are crafted to reflect the characters' emotions and the underlying tensions in their relationships.

**KALU and SUNANDA's Relationship:** Their dialogue reveals the complexity of their relationship, with SUNANDA expressing her dissatisfaction and KALU's defensive response.

**KALU and Monika's Connection**: Their phone conversation is friendly but hints at deeper feelings and unresolved issues.

**DAYA BABU's Loneliness**: His fairy tale and final monologue poignantly reflect his grief and isolation.

**Visual and Symbolic Elements**: The fairy tale can be visually depicted through DAYA BABU's storytelling, contrasting with the reality of the characters' lives.

**Tone and Mood**: The screenplay maintains a contemplative and introspective tone, with moments of warmth and underlying sadness.

This screenplay offers a rich exploration of the characters and their relationships, providing opportunities for emotional performances and visual storytelling.

# Scene 26

**INT. KALU AND SUNANDA'S BATHROOM - MORNING**

Camera opens up panning over outside of Kalu's house moving in focuses on Sunanda

SUNANDA is dyeing her hair. KALU passes by.

**SUNANDA:** You also dye your hair black, more than half of it is white.

**KALU:** (Refusing) Why to use artificial colours on something that is natural? Anyway, on whom God has poured a stock of black color, anything white, even if it is tilak, will look better.

**SUNANDA:** (Consoling) Why do you keep getting frustrated about your dark complexion? How many people have a pure heart like yours? You look very cute.

**KALU:** (Exhaling) Yes, it's right. It has been fifteen years since the one who used to care about my complexion, passed away.

They discuss plans for the evening with friends and family.

**INT. KALU AND SUNANDA'S LIVING ROOM - NIGHT**

KALU, SUNANDA, GAURAV, and SOPHIA enjoy a sumptuous dinner and gossip.

**SOPHIA:** (Looking at the clock) It's half past eleven, now we must go to the hotel, otherwise we will have to spend the night on the street.

**GAURAV:** (Enjoying dessert) Enough, now let's leave soon.

**KALU & SUNANDA:** (Together) What is so nice in the hotel that you can't stay at our house? Have breakfast in the morning and then go.

**SOPHIA:** You have not left any space in our stomach. With already overeating, now we will directly have dinner tomorrow night.

After they left Kalu and Sunanda started preparing for going to bed.

**INT. KALU AND SUNANDA'S BEDROOM - LATE NIGHT**

Phone RINGS. KALU answers. It's CHANDA, panicked.

**CHANDA:** Someone has kidnapped Pratyush on his way back from the private hospital around 9 o'clock. They are demanding one crore in ransom. They have instructed not to inform the police, else they are threatening to kill him.

**KALU:** (Reassuring) Don't worry, nothing will happen to Pratyush. We'll get him out anyhow. Be patient and stop crying and encourage everyone. I am talking to Nehal who is home minister in Maharashtra govt these days.

SUNANDA overhears and starts calling her brother, a senior police officer for the help. He responds in affirmation.

**KALU:** (talks with Nehal on phone) We need your help as my brother in law Dr Pratyush has been kidnapped at Patna while returning from his hospital.

**NEHAL:** Don't worry. I am immediately calling Chief minister of Bihar and let assured, nothing will happen to him. After that I will also have talk with Chanda. Please share her phone number.

**KALU:** So nice of you! Thanks.

**INT. VARIOUS LOCATIONS - NEXT TWO DAYS**

Chaos ensues. News channels and newspapers cover the kidnapping. Pressure builds on the kidnappers.

**INT. KALU AND SUNANDA'S LIVING ROOM - THIRD DAY - MORNING**

KALU receives a call informing that PRATYUSH has been released.

**KALU:** (Relieved) He's safe. They left him at a deserted place on the highway.

**SUNANDA:** (Concerned) But his face and body language will be terrorised for a long time.

They discuss the whispers of ransom and the deteriorating law and order situation.

**FADE TO BLACK.**

**Themes and Notes:**

This screenplay captures the events and emotions of Chapter 26, focusing on the relationships between the characters and the tension of the kidnapping incident.

**KALU and SUNANDA's Relationship:** Their dialogue in the bathroom reveals their playful and supportive relationship.

Dinner with Friends: The evening with GAURAV and SOPHIA provides a contrast to the later tension, showing the warmth and camaraderie between the friends.

**Kidnapping Incident:** The kidnapping of PRATYUSH and the subsequent chaos are depicted with urgency and concern, reflecting the societal issues at play.

**Visual and Symbolic Elements:** The contrast between the joyful dinner and the terror of the kidnapping can be visually depicted to emphasize the unpredictability of life.

**Tone and Mood:** The screenplay moves from light-hearted and warm to tense and concerned, reflecting the sudden shift in circumstances.

**Social Commentary:** The screenplay subtly comments on societal issues such as law and order, corruption, and fear, providing a broader context to the personal story.

This screenplay offers a blend of personal relationships and societal concerns, providing opportunities for emotional performances and a reflection on broader themes.

❏❏

# Scene 27

**INT. KALU AND SUNANDA'S LIVING ROOM - SUNDAY AFTERNOON**

Camera opens up panning over Kalu's door focuses on Monika knocking the door.

MONIKA arrives and agrees to stay at SUNANDA's house on her insistence. KALU is pushed into the children's room as the two ladies decide to occupy master bedroom.

**INT. KALU AND SUNANDA'S LIVING ROOM - EVENING**

MONIKA, KALU, and SUNANDA enjoy games, singing, and political discussions. They reminisce about old times.

**INT. KALU AND SUNANDA'S LIVING ROOM - FIFTH DAY**

MONIKA leaves for Delhi, promising to return in a few years.

**INT. KALU AND SUNANDA'S DINING ROOM - NIGHT**

SUNANDA reveals to KALU that MONIKA has filed for divorce.

**SUNANDA:** You know, Monika ji has filed for divorce from her husband, and now the decision is going to come in a few months.

**KALU:** (Surprised) What? Monika told you this? What happened between them that it reached to the point of divorce?

**SUNANDA:** No, refused to give a reason, citing privacy. You may ask her as she is your friend. She may tell you.

**KALU:** You never know. She never shared about her strained relationship with husband. But I had a gut feeling of something wrong as she avoided talking about her husband though talking lot about Makalu. I'll do so only after final judgement comes out.

They discuss the situation, expressing concern for MONIKA and her son, MAKALU.


**KALU:** Has she told you anything about Makalu, her son? Who will take care of him?


**SUNANDA:** Nothing to worry about her son. He is already living with her and Vikram ji has no time out of his business to look after Makalu. He has already filed an agreement regarding this in court.


**KALU:** It'll be fair. Atleast, she will have some one to live with.


**INT. KALU AND SUNANDA'S BEDROOM - NIGHT**

KALU and SUNANDA lie awake, each lost in thought.

**KALU'S THOUGHTS:** (V.O.) How much loneliness she has suffered in her life! She could not rely on any one to share her grief throughout her life. She was in habbit of sharing all goodies with me but never her grievances since Childhood. If I call her now, she might take it as intrusion into her personal life for which I have no right. It'll be fair to call her regarding this only after divorce is final.

(Love buried in a pile of extinguished ashes takes special care that it does not blow into and become gritty in the eyes of beloved)

**SUNANDA'S THOUGHTS:** (V.O.) How can someone remain so isolated even after living together for twenty-five years? Millions of thanks to God that I got such an understanding and caring husband. He spends whole night awake changing posture when I am in little bit of trouble as he is doing now for his childhood friend. So kind hearted person he is!

**INT. KALU AND SUNANDA'S KITCHEN - NEXT MORNING**

SUNANDA wakes KALU up as he is sleeping till late morning and prepares breakfast as well as lunch to be taken to office. She asks him to call MONIKA and checking on her regularly.

**KALU:** (Smiling) You will not have any problem with this, will you? After all, you too must have a woman's heart.

**SUNANDA:** (Firmly) Damn, I'm not a jealous and suspicious woman. I have full faith on you.

**KALU:** Think it again. She is going to have divorce too.

**SUNANDA:** Hiss! I have no problem if something cooks between you two. I'll accept her as my elder sister.

**KALU:** Ha ha ha!

They tease each other playfully as KALU leaves for work.

**FADE TO BLACK.**

**Themes and Notes:**

This screenplay captures the emotional complexity of relationships, trust, and the impact of life-changing decisions.

**KALU and SUNANDA's Relationship:** Their dialogue and interactions reveal a deep understanding and trust between them. They are supportive of each other and of their friend MONIKA.

**MONIKA's Divorce:** The revelation of MONIKA's divorce serves as a central plot point, leading to reflections on love, loneliness, and companionship. It also prompts KALU and SUNANDA to consider their own relationship.

**Emotional Complexity:** The characters grapple with complex emotions, including surprise, concern, empathy, and introspection. Their internal thoughts provide insight into their feelings and reactions.

**Visual and Symbolic Elements:** The shifting settings, from the lively living room to the contemplative bedroom, visually represent the characters' emotional journeys.

**Tone and Mood:** The screenplay moves from joyful and playful to thoughtful and introspective, reflecting the characters' changing emotions and the gravity of MONIKA's situation.

**Social Commentary:** The screenplay subtly explores societal attitudes toward divorce, relationships, and gender roles, providing a nuanced perspective on these issues.

This screenplay offers a rich exploration of human emotions and relationships, providing opportunities for character-driven storytelling and emotional performances.

❑❑

## Scene 28

**INT. MONIKA'S LIVING ROOM - MORNING**

Camera panning over outside of Monika's bungalow focuses on Monika and Makalu inside.

MONIKA is preparing to leave for court. MAKALU, her son, confronts her with questions about the impending divorce.

**MAKALU:** Today you two will be separated forever. will I never see Papa again?

**MONIKA:** (Struggling) No son, it will not be like that. Even after today he will be your father and whenever you want to meet him, you can..

**MAKALU:** But Mumma! Now he will be free to remarry. With new spouse coming in, he will have more time constraints to think of meeting me.

He is already having little time to spare for me.

**MONIKA:** I am already strained about such complxities. Till now, I tolerated your father only because of you. Even today, I will be very happy if you want to live with your father.

**MAKALU:** No Mumma! No question of changing my decision of staying with you. Just a query which I wanted to check with you. I have never seen you happy and to me you appeared a very serious boring person but I have seen your laughing photos with your friends and during your trip to India. I can understand that the bitterness of conjugal life has damaged softness of your persona a lot. While dealing with me, you changes to so nice, loving person.

They discuss the situation, with MAKALU expressing concerns and MONIKA reassuring him.

**INT. COURTROOM - DAY**

MONIKA waits for her turn, lost in memories of her marriage to VIKRAM.

**FLASHBACK:**

**INT. MONIKA AND VIKRAM'S LIVING ROOM - VARIOUS TIMES**

Scenes from MONIKA and VIKRAM's marriage play out, showing the initial happiness, VIKRAM's introverted personality, the birth of MAKALU, and the growing distance between them.

**MONIKA:** How many times I have to apologize before you without any fault of mine. Your male ego will never let you realise your mistakes. I am talking to you in futility as you will remain silent and ignore me as always. I thought you would improve after birth of Makalu but nothing changed except a few queries about Makalu and daily house hold needs. You never showed any intimacy with me and thought providing us basic and luxurious amenities are your only responsibilities towards family. Initially I thought it was because of your introvert nature but I have found you comfortably talking a lot alongwith cracking jokes when you are among your friends and their wives. Probably I am not of your choice so never developed any intimate feelings for me except formal conjugal life.

Vikram silently walks out of conversation without giving any reply.

**MONIKA:** Same treatment again. Now it's too much. Enough is enough. I'll file a divorce petition tomorrow as Makalu also grew up now.

**BACK TO PRESENT: (following interruption by Judge's voice)**

### INT. COURTROOM - DAY

The JUDGE addresses MONIKA and VIKRAM.

**JUDGE:** You guys have taken the final decision of separation or if there is still any scope for reconciliation, the court is ready to give more time.

**MONIKA:** Yes Me Lord!, I have made up my mind. I'm not ready to stay with him even a day more.

**JUDGE:** (to Vikram) And sir! You also giving consent.

**VIKRAM:** Yes, Me Lord!.

**JUDGE:** The divorce is granted. The child Makalu will live in her mother's custody but she will allow father to meet his son whenever he wishes.

MONIKA and VIKRAM exchange final words and glances.

**VIKRAM:** (To MAKALU) Whenever you remember father, feel free to come, son. My doors will always be open for you.

**MONIKA:** (Silently) Khuda Hafiz.

**VIKRAM:** (to Monika) Thanks for spending so much time with me. Please forgive me. I couldn't give you what you deserved but it is all past now. Try to lead better life in future and if possible search for a better match. May God bless you peace of mind and happiness.

MONIKA gives back empty smile to Vikram.

### INT. RESTAURANT - NIGHT

MONIKA and MAKALU celebrate with dinner. MONIKA appears happy and relieved.

### INT. MONIKA'S BEDROOM - NIGHT

MONIKA reflects on the day's events, grappling with mixed emotions.

**MONIKA'S THOUGHTS:** (V.O.) Is it right to get rid of the trap of a relationship by getting divorced? But will it be able to end the daily solitude? The only happiness is that a sad story has come to an end.

**FADE TO BLACK.**

**Themes and Notes:**

This screenplay captures the emotional complexity of divorce, relationships, and self-reflection.

**MONIKA's Journey:** The chapter follows MONIKA's journey from confronting her son's questions to reflecting on her marriage and finally gaining her independence through divorce.

**MAKALU's Concerns:** MAKALU's questions and concerns provide insight into the impact of divorce on children and the challenges of navigating these conversations.

**Flashbacks:** The flashbacks to MONIKA and VIKRAM's marriage provide context and depth to their relationship, showing the progression from happiness to distance and indifference.

**Emotional Complexity:** The characters grapple with complex emotions, including fear, relief, uncertainty, and introspection. MONIKA's internal thoughts provide insight into her feelings and reactions.

**Visual and Symbolic Elements:** The shifting settings, from the intimate living room to the formal courtroom, visually represent the characters' emotional journeys.

**Tone and Mood:** The screenplay moves from tense and confrontational to reflective and introspective, reflecting the characters' changing emotions and the gravity of the situation.

**Social Commentary:** The screenplay explores societal attitudes toward marriage, divorce, and relationships, providing a nuanced perspective on these issues.

This screenplay offers a rich exploration of human emotions and relationships, providing opportunities for character-driven storytelling and emotional performances. It also provides a thoughtful examination of the complexities of divorce and its impact on all involved.

❑❑

# Scene 29

**INT. WOMEN'S HOSTEL - DAY**

Camera panning over women's hostel converges to guest room and focuses on Ruchi and Pulkit alternate while they talk

RUCHI and PULKIT are having a conversation about their relationship and studies.

**RUCHI:** Nowadays you rarely come to see me. Is there anything special or have you found someone else?

**PULKIT:** No way!, this study has decided to become your sautan. It doesn't give me time to meet you.

**RUCHI:** Why not? It's only you who have to study hard otherwise I pass by cheating.

Though I am not topper like you, but my score is not too bad.

**PULKIT**: Examiners award you girl extra marks for your look only. Anyway have you talked with parents about our relationship?

**RUCHI**: Yes, I talked with my Papa and he has not only given green signal but also assured of talking to your father about us. But I have instructed him not to hurry for the marriage. And what about you, Mr! Any progress from your side.

**PULKIT**: That's great that you already pleaded for late marriage. We will marry after finishing our study and getting good placement in job. I also had talk with my mother. She also likes you and now your Papa will talk to my dad and the two friends will surely agree to become relatives.

They banter about their relationship, studies, and future plans. They agree to depart now before girl's hostel bell rings announcing end of visiting hours.

### INT. KALU AND SUNANDA'S LIVING ROOM - DAY

VINOD calls KALU to discuss RUCHI and PULKIT's relationship.

**VINOD:** I am asking for the hand of your son Pulkit for my daughter Ruchi.

**KALU:** Wow, what could be better! We both will become relatives from friends. Have you taken permission from Sushma Bhabhi?

**VINOD:** Yes, she also agreed after initial iffs and buts. She is right here with me.

**SUSHMA:** Hello Bhai saheb! You also ask from Sunanda didi though she knows everything from before and given her consent. But children are not in hurry to get married. They want it to be solemnised after they pass out and get their jobs.

**SUNANDA:** That's fine, Didi. We will get time to arrange Shreya's marriage before Pulkit's.

**SUSHMA:** You talk to Shreya about her marriage plan today only. If she agrees for arranged marriage, then we'll also search for her suitable match.

**KALU:** Please both of you make a plan to visit Hyderabad in near future so that we can discuss in details. I will get consent from my father and other relatives though I am sure they will not object as the two families know each other for such a long time.

They exchange congratulations and agree to meet soon at Hyderabad.

**INT. SHREYA'S ROOM - DAY**

SHREYA picks up phone seeing Mummy's call.

**SUNANDA:** Hello Shreya! If you are free, I want to discuss about your marriage plan.

**SHREYA:** No Mummy! I'll not marry and remain single.

**SUNANDA:** PULKIT AND RUCHI are in love with each other and we have agreed for their marriage. So, if you have any love story, please share with me now.

**SHREYA:** Mummy, I fell in love with a boy from Hyderabad, Siddhiraman, during my schooling and it still continues secretly.

**SUNANDA:** Have you met his family and are they ready for this relationship?

**SHREYA:** Yes, I have met his parents. They like me and ready to accept me as their daughter in law.

**SUNANDA:** Then, ask Siddhi to arrange our meeting with his parents so that we can discuss the marriage plan with them.

**SHREYA:** Thanks, Mummy! You and Papa are too good. I was initially afraid that you will not agree for this east and south relationship and even if you two agree, Dada Ji and bua-chachas will object to such type of love marriage in our family. That's why I initially said I will not marry at all. Sorry for that, Mummy. When you informed me about Pulkit and Ruchi, then I got the courage to open my secret. Siddhi and I have decided not to marry without your permission and remain unmarried lifelong. Thanks God! I'll talk to Papa later on in the evening.

**SUNANDA:** Your generation is too selfish. You pour love on your parents when your demand is fulfilled.

**INT. KALU AND SUNANDA'S BEDROOM - NIGHT**

KALU and SUNANDA discuss their children's relationships and prepare for the upcoming meetings.

Shreya informs that Siddhi has arranged their meeting with his parents next Sunday and she is also coming in morning same day. She shared her flight ticket too.

**KALU:** See how much our daughter is in a hurry to leave parent's house and go to husband's house. Let's also prepare ourselves for sending her off otherwise we will sink in ocean of tears at that time.

**SUNANDA:** You will cry more, you see.

They reflect on their children's happiness and go to sleep.

**FADE TO BLACK**

**Themes and Notes:**

This chapter focuses on the relationships of the younger generation and the supportive and progressive attitudes of the parents.

**RUCHI and PULKIT's Relationship:** The opening scene establishes the romantic relationship between RUCHI and PULKIT, showcasing their playful banter and mutual understanding.

**Parental Support:** The conversations between VINOD, KALU, and SUNANDA highlight the parents' willingness to support their children's choices and the importance of communication and consent.

**SHREYA's Secret Love:** SHREYA's revelation of her secret relationship with SIDDHIRAMAN adds a layer of complexity and shows SUNANDA's understanding and supportive nature.

**Emotional Complexity:** The characters navigate complex emotions, including excitement, anxiety, joy, and anticipation. The dialogues capture the nuances of their feelings and reactions.

**Visual and Symbolic Elements:** The shifting settings, from the hostel to the family homes, visually represent the characters' emotional journeys and the progression of their relationships.

**Tone and Mood:** The screenplay moves from playful and romantic to reflective and supportive, reflecting the characters' changing emotions and the importance of family and love.

**Social Commentary:** The screenplay explores modern relationships, parental support, and the importance of communication and understanding in family dynamics.

This screenplay offers a heartwarming exploration of love, family, and relationships, providing opportunities for character-driven storytelling and emotional performances. It also provides a thoughtful examination of the complexities of modern relationships and the supportive role of parents.

❑❑

# Scene 30

**INT. KALU AND SUNANDA'S LIVING ROOM - DAY**

Camera opens up panning over living room focuses on Sunanda.

SUNANDA is feeling the absence of her daughter SHREYA, who has been married six months ago. KALU tries to console her.

**SUNANDA:** Even after six months of Shreya's departure, it seems as if she has gone only yesterday.

**KALU:** Earlier also she was living away from us in Poona. Then what happened that it has become so bitter?

They decide to visit SHREYA's in-laws.

**INT. SHREYA'S IN-LAWS' DINING ROOM - NIGHT**

Everyone is enjoying a meal together, praising the Hyderabadi Biryani and discussing family matters.

**MRS. JAYANTHI:(pointing towards Mr Ganeshan)** It is a wonder of his and your daughter Shreya's hands. Daughter-in-law and father-in-law made it together.

**SHREYA:** What mom! You are making me climb the shrubs. The truth is, you people are so gentle that you always praise me ignoring my mistakes.

They discuss visiting each other's homes and celebrate the family connections.

**INT. KALU AND SUNANDA'S BEDROOM - NIGHT**

KALU and SUNANDA reflect on their visit and SUNANDA reveals that SHREYA is pregnant.

**KALU:** So are we going to be grandparents? You didn't tell me earlier.

**SUNANDA:** She told me the good news only this evening, after the tests confirmed it.

They decide to congratulate the family in the morning.

## INT. HOTEL BALLROOM - DAY (NINE MONTHS LATER)

A grand celebration for the arrival of SHREYA's baby. Relatives and friends from both families are present, including DAYA BABU, CHANDA, VINOD, NEHAL, and others.

Mr Ganeshan, Mrs JAYANTHI, Mr Siddhiraman and their relatives are too happy to see cordial behaviour of Shreya's extended family who have come in such a large number from so distant place like Patna to Hyderabad just to give blessings to the new member of their family.

**MR. GANESHAN:** (to Daya Babu with folded hands) I am really overwhelmed by your presence in this function. You took pain to travel after so many years of confining yourself to Patna just to honour my invitation.

**KALU and SUNANDA:** Yes, we too are lucky to have him with us and our granddaughter should be given the credit for the same.

**MRS. JAYANTHI:** People differentiating on the basis of regionalism, language and caste should come and see how lovely this gathering is. Just cross the boundary of inhibition and plenty of love is awaiting to welcome you.

Everyone is overjoyed, and the atmosphere is festive. Both hosts and guests are pleased with the excellent arrangements.

**INT. KALU'S LIVING ROOM - DAY (NEXT MORNING)**

VINOD and CHANDA have a family lunch with KALU's extended family. They discuss the marriage of RUCHI and PULKIT.

**PULKIT:** Please don't hurry. Give us time to finish our study and get our placement.

**DAYA BABU:** My wish to see your marriage should not remain unfulfilled.

**RUCHI** : Okay Dada Ji! As per your wish we are ready to get married next year before monsoon. Now Papa and uncle can fix the date of engagement as per convenience of all.


PULKIT and Ruchi touch feet of all elders starting from Dada Ji and ending with Siddhi and Shreya.

**INT. KALU'S LIVING ROOM - EVENING**

MONIKA calls to congratulate KALU on becoming a maternal grandfather and shares the news of MAKALU opening a cafe in Canada.


Everyone congratulates each other, and PULKIT has an intimate conversation with MAKALU, inviting him to India. On demand of Makalu he hands over the mobile to Ruchi.


**RUCHI:** Makalu, why don't you come to India? This time, along with your mother, you also come and meet all of us.

**MAKALU:** Oh sure! I'll accompany mumma during her next visit to

India. But you and Pulkit plan to visit Canada.

**PULKIT:** Rest assured, our honeymoon will be in Canada and Ruchi is also nodding her head in affirmation.

They share phone numbers and promise to keep in touch.

**FADE TO BLACK**

**Themes and Notes:**

This chapter focuses on family connections, celebrations, and the joy of new beginnings.

**Family Bonds:** The screenplay emphasizes the strong bonds between family members, including in-laws, extended family, and friends. The interactions are warm, loving, and supportive.

**Celebrations and Milestones:** The chapter includes significant life events, such as the birth of a child and the planning of a wedding. These events work as the family get together and provide opportunities for joyous gatherings.

**Cultural Connections:** The screenplay showcases the blending of different cultures and traditions, as seen in the Hyderabadi Biryani and the interactions between family members from different regions.

**Emotional Complexity:** The characters experience a range of emotions, from nostalgia and longing to joy and excitement. The dialogues and interactions capture these nuanced feelings.

**Visual and Symbolic Elements:** The settings, from the family homes to the grand hotel ballroom, visually represent the characters' emotional journeys and the importance of family and tradition.

**Tone and Mood:** The screenplay is warm, celebratory, and heartfelt, reflecting the characters' love for one another and their shared joy in life's milestones.

**Social Commentary:** The screenplay subtly addresses issues of language, region, and caste, showing how love and understanding can transcend these barriers.

This screenplay offers a rich exploration of family, love, and tradition, providing opportunities for heartfelt storytelling and emotional performances. It also provides a thoughtful examination of cultural connections and the importance of family in shaping our lives.

# Scene 31

### INT. UPSCALE HOTEL IN MAHABALI PURAM - AUDITORIUM - DAY

Camera opens up panning over the hotel and moving in towards auditorium covering groups of women focuses on Lakshmi.

Sunanda's old college friends are gathered for a reunion. They're enjoying various activities, and LAKSHMI insists that SUNANDA must sing.


**LAKSHMI:** No Sunanda! You have to sing too. In the days of college, we have heard song in your melodious voice. Don't throw tantrums like a famous singer today.


The crowd chants SUNANDA's name, and she sings a beautiful song.


### INT. LOBBY TO HOTEL DINING HALL - DAY

The friends are having lunch, reminiscing about old times and teasing each other about their husbands and families. Some are walking towards dining hall.

**VIMLA:** Sunanda, in what thoughts are you lost? You must be remembering your dear husband.

**SUNANDA:** Where all are going? Probably music session has ended.

**VIMLA:** Oh yes my beautiful doll! They are going for lunch and we should also move fast.

They discuss the evening's fancy dress competition and head to their rooms after lunch.

### INT. SUNANDA'S HOTEL ROOM - DAY

SUNANDA receives a call from her husband, KALU.

**KALU:** How are you, is everything fine? You must have taken your sumptuous lunch. Must be having a lot of fun there and here I am eating dry roti dal remembering you.

**SUNANDA:** Everything is going great. I would have been deprived of such a good stay, if I would have cancelled my trip on your request. Sometimes, it's good not to heed to husband's advice.Is not it? You consider me a cook only that's why remembering me seeing the food.

**KALU:** Believe it or not. I miss you every moment since you have gone.

**SUNANDA:** Don't try to be extra romantic. It looks odd. I will come back by tomorrow evening. I am going to participate in today's fancy dress competition in the make up of a joker. How is the idea?

**KALU:** Excellent! Just rehearse the dialogue delivery. Get your performance video recorded in your mobile so that I can see it later.

They flirt and tease each other and bid good bye after few minutes.

### INT. SUNANDA'S HOTEL ROOM - LATER

SUNANDA prepares her Joker costume and practices her dialogue in front of the mirror. Satisfied, she lays down to rest.

### INT. SUNANDA'S DREAM - AFTERNOON

SUNANDA dreams of floating in the sky as an angel, then being drawn into a dark tunnel by a sweet tune. She hears KALU's voice calling her back, but she is unable to reach out to him.

**SUNANDA:** (Shouting) No, I don't want to go away from you. Do anything, take me out of this tunnel and take me back with you, please.

She wakes up, crying and disoriented.

**INT. SUNANDA'S HOTEL ROOM – EVENING**

SUNANDA splashes water on her face and orders tea to calm herself. She checks the time and realizes she needs to get ready for the fancy dress competition. Soon she also gets alert from reception to proceed for fancy dress program.

**FADE TO BLACK**

**Themes and Notes:**

This chapter focuses on the joy of reconnection, the importance of self-expression, and the unsettling nature of dreams.

**Reconnection with Friends:** The screenplay highlights the joy and nostalgia of reconnecting with old friends. The characters' interactions are filled with warmth, humor, and shared memories.

**Self-Expression and Playfulness:** The characters engage in singing, dancing, and dressing up, embracing their playful sides. SUNANDA's decision to dress as a Joker symbolizes her willingness to step outside her usual role and have fun.

**The Unsettling Dream:** SUNANDA's dream adds a mysterious and unsettling element to the story. The dream's imagery and emotions hint at deeper fears and desires, creating a contrast with the joyful reunion.

**Relationship Dynamics:** The interactions between SUNANDA and KALU, both in person and over the phone, reveal a loving and teasing relationship. Their banter adds depth to their characters and provides insight into their marriage.

Visual and Symbolic Elements: The screenplay includes visually engaging scenes, such as SUNANDA's dream and her preparation for the fancy dress competition. The Joker costume and the dark tunnel in the dream can be interpreted symbolically, adding layers of meaning to the story.

**Tone and Mood:** The screenplay is joyful and nostalgic, with moments of humor and playfulness. The dream sequence adds a touch of mystery and unease, creating a contrast that adds complexity to the story.

**Character Development:** The chapter provides insight into SUNANDA's character, revealing her playful side, her love for her husband, and her underlying fears and desires.

This screenplay offers a rich exploration of friendship, self-expression, and the complexities of dreams and relationships. It provides opportunities for engaging performances, visually striking scenes, and thoughtful storytelling.

# Scene 32

**INT. HOTEL AUDITORIUM - NIGHT**

Camera opens up panning over the lobby of hotel and moving in towards auditorium focuses on to the stage and then pans back to show audience.

The auditorium is decorated for a fancy dress competition. Friends and guests are gathered, and the competition begins with various humorous acts, including that of a beggar woman, then a policeman, later a chanting Baba followed by a leader, a witch, and a Tantrik.

**INT. HOTEL AUDITORIUM - LATER**

SUNANDA, dressed as a Joker, takes the stage. She entertains the audience with her antics and then delivers a heartfelt monologue.

**SUNANDA:** Namaskar, Adab, Sat Sri Akal! Brothers, sisters, boys and girls!!! Recognized me? Yes, got it right. I am the one who makes you all laugh...... Whatever you call me, I will love any name given by you. The joker is always ready to do whatever I can to bring smile on your face. If I ever be silent, it'll be in such a way that you will continue to applaud by endless clapping. Now the play begins... What is happening to my voice. I am losing consciousness. Kalu! Shreya!! Pulkit!!! Where are you all. Someone is calling me from other side of light. I'll have to go. Oh! Eternal peace that side.

Her voice falters, and she collapses on stage, whispering goodbye.

**SUNANDA:** Goodbye friends, goodbye!

The audience applauds, thinking it's part of the act. But when SUNANDA doesn't move at all, panic sets in.

**INT. HOTEL LOBBY - NIGHT**

**DR. NISCHAL SHARMA** examines SUNANDA and announces her death. Friends are stunned and grief-stricken.

**INT. CHENNAI AIRPORT - NIGHT**

KALU, SUNANDA's husband, arrives and proceeds towards Mahabali Puram on cab.

**INT. MORTUARY- MORNING**

Reaching Mahabalipuram Kalu knows about wife's death. He condoles and pays his last respects in mortuary and arranges for her body to be sent to Hyderabad.

**INT. HYDERABAD AIRPORT - DAY**

KALU, PULKIT, SHREYA, SIDDHI, and others await SUNANDA's body. They share the incident and console each other.

**SHREYA:** Take care of yourself, Papa, otherwise we will break apart. You will have to play the role of our mother too after she is no more.

**KALU:** You are saying the right thing, but my strength, my courage was only your mother. Without her, my existence has remained like a desolate ruin.

Every one gathered pays homage with wet eyes to the dead body.

### INT. KALU'S HOUSE - DAY

The family performs the cremation and other rituals, supporting each other through the period of grief.

### INT. KALU'S HOUSE - LATER

Life slowly returns to normal, but KALU is left alone with his loneliness after Shrya and Siddhi have to return on their duty after 3weeks and when he starts going to office, Pulkit also proceeds to join his college on father's insistence.

**FADE TO BLACK**

**Themes and Notes:**

This chapter focuses on the themes of performance, unexpected loss, grief, and the process of healing.

**Performance and Reality:** The chapter begins with a lively and humorous fancy dress competition, where the line between performance and reality is blurred. SUNANDA's collapse on stage is initially perceived as part of her act, highlighting the power of performance to shape perception.

**Unexpected Loss:** SUNANDA's sudden death shocks her friends and family, turning a joyful reunion into a tragic event. Her death is portrayed with sensitivity and realism, capturing the disbelief, grief, and confusion that often accompany unexpected loss.

**Grief and Healing:** The chapter explores the process of grieving and healing, showing how the family comes together to support each other. The rituals and ceremonies provide a structure for their grief, allowing them to honor SUNANDA's memory and begin to move forward.

**Loneliness and Resilience:** KALU's loneliness after SUNANDA's death is a poignant reminder of the void left by her absence. His gradual return to normalcy reflects the resilience of the human spirit and the necessity of moving on.

**Visual and Symbolic Elements:** The chapter includes visually engaging scenes, such as the fancy dress competition and the rituals surrounding SUNANDA's death. The Joker costume symbolizes SUNANDA's playful spirit and her desire to bring joy to others, adding depth to her character.

**Tone and Mood:** The screenplay shifts from joyful and humorous to somber and reflective, mirroring the emotional journey of the characters. The tone is respectful and empathetic, capturing the complexity of grief and loss.

**Character Development:** The chapter provides insight into SUNANDA's character and her relationships with her friends and family. Her death serves as a catalyst for the characters to reflect on their own lives and values.

This screenplay offers a rich exploration of performance, unexpected loss, grief, and healing. It provides opportunities for powerful performances, visually engaging scenes, and thoughtful storytelling. The emotional depth and complexity of the story make it a compelling and resonant narrative.

# Scene 33

**INT. EGYPT - PYRAMIDS - DAY**

Camera opens up panning over pyramids in Egypt and focuses on Monika.

MONIKA, on vacation near the pyramids of Egypt, receives a call from her son MAKALU.

**MAKALU:** Mummy, this time on vacation I will take you on a trip to Europe. Every time you go out with friends. Sometimes give time to your son too.

**MONIKA:** Yes, of course. Will return on Sunday after finishing a week's vacation. Then leave may be available after six months.

They agree to plan a trip during Christmas.

**INT. KALU'S KITCHEN - DAY**

KALU is experimenting with cooking, trying to make different delicious dishes. Slowly he's becoming a capable cook and feels Sugandha's presence by his side, guiding him during cooking about appropriate proportion of salt and spices to be added. This way he is trying to spend time after returning from office.

**INT. KALU'S LIVING ROOM - MORNING/EVENING**

KALU sits and talks near SUNANDA's picture, chatting with her as if she's really there. Some times he himself doubts whether he is losing mental balance or turning lunatic.

**INT. KALU'S OFFICE - DAY**

MONIKA calls KALU, checking on him and offering encouragement.

**MONIKA:** Hi Kalu! How are you? Don't tell me 'fine'. I myself have gone through these difficult moments time and again. So I know how tough it is for you these days. Whether you like it or not, I will call you frequently to repay the good gesture of yours and Sunanda after my divorce, supporting by calling at regular intervals to mitigate my sorrow.

**KALU:** Your words give me solace but how can I forget my life partner Sunanda who spent so many years with me. I am habituated of her constant accompany.

**MONIKA:** You don't have to try to forget Sunanda at all. Just be happy remembering the good times you have spent with her. But try not to remain sad because she can't have peace if you remain in agony. Explore reasons and occasions to laugh just to make her soul happy as she always toiled hard to keep you and her children joyful. Think in this way though it is easier to say than to do.


**KALU:** The bravery with which you have faced the tragedy of a mismatched marriage earlier and are now facing the difficulties of a divorced woman is commendable. It gives me immense inspiration and strength to negotiate through the tough times.


They share their troubles and find comfort in each other's words. After call is over -


**KALU:** (to himself) These calls from friends and relatives keep me engaged and are of profound help to break the monotony of my life and divert my attention. Even in -laws keep on calling me at regular intervals and asking me to visit their house and spend some weeks with them. But how it's possible leaving my office for too long. Mr Ganeshan and Mrs JAYANTHI are kind enough to come to meet me quite often as well as making phone calls to enquire about my health. I am lucky to have co-operation from every near and dear otherwise who cares for other in this selfish world.

**INT. KALU'S LIVING ROOM - DAY**

KALU remembers the promise of the video from LAKSHMI and VIMLA. He calls them, and they apologize for not sending it, fearing it would agonize him.

**LAKSHMI:** I am sending you the video but after a promise that You will maintain courage. Understand that no one can avoid the eternal rule of nature. Call me or any friend of Sunanda without hesitation for any kind of help.

**KALU:** In these days, I have learned to compromise with the situation and have kept a heavy stone over my heart. Nothing will happen to a stone-hearted person like me.

They express gratitude and support for each other.

**INT. KALU'S LIVING ROOM - LATER**

KALU watches the video of SUNANDA's last days, feeling both comfort and pain. He sees her last-minute call to him and the kids, and her saying that someone on the other side of the light is calling her.

**KALU:** (to himself) No body knows whether she was referring to God in her last words or it was part of her dialogues. The mystery will always remain unsolved.

**FADE TO BLACK**

**Themes and Notes:**

This chapter focuses on the themes of coping with loss, finding support, and the power of memory.

**Coping with Loss:** KALU's journey through grief continues as he finds ways to cope with SUNANDA's absence. From cooking to talking to her picture, he's finding ways to keep her memory alive.

**Finding Support:** The chapter emphasizes the importance of support from friends and family. MONIKA'S encouragement, the GANESAN couple's affection, and the video from LAKSHMI and VIMLA all help KALU navigate his grief.

**The Power of Memory:** The video of SUNANDA's last days serves as a poignant reminder of her presence and the love they shared. It's both painful and comforting, reflecting the complex nature of memory.

**Character Development:** KALU's character continues to evolve as he learns to live without SUNANDA. His strength and resilience are evident, as is his vulnerability.

**Visual and Symbolic Elements:** The video of SUNANDA's last moments is a powerful visual element, capturing her essence and providing a tangible connection to her memory. KALU's cooking symbolizes his attempt to create something new in his life.

**Tone and Mood:** The tone is reflective and introspective, exploring the emotional landscape of grief and healing. There's a sense of hope and resilience, tempered by the ongoing pain of loss.

**Dialogue and Interaction:** The conversations between KALU and MONIKA, and KALU and LAKSHMI, provide insight into their relationships and the shared experience of loss. The dialogue is heartfelt and authentic, reflecting their mutual support and understanding.

This screenplay offers a thoughtful exploration of grief, support, and memory. It provides opportunities for emotional performances and visually engaging scenes. The complexity of the characters and their relationships adds depth to the story, making it a compelling and resonant narrative.

❏❏

# Scene 34

**INT. VINOD AND SUSHMA'S LIVING ROOM - DAY**

Camera panning over a bungalow moves into living room and focuses on Sushma.

VINOD and SUSHMA discuss their plan to visit Kalu in Hyderabad.

**SUSHMA:** We will stay with him, not in any hotel and try to lift his spirits. I'll cook food myself to bring a change in his taste so that his mood gets elevated.

**VINOD:** I will also try to create an atmosphere of laughter and happiness with my banters. You take care. We should not start our debate there. Such a long ceasefire will hurt you but there is no other option available.

**SUSHMA:** Then you will have indigestion. Even three bottles of Hajmola may not be enough to digest the food without quarrelling. But one thing is clear that we will never mention about Sunanda otherwise his wounds will be refreshed.

**VINOD :** (bending forward in respect) Totally agree !

They laugh and finalize their plan.

**INT. KALU'S LIVING ROOM- DAY**

After ringing of door bell, KALU opens the door to find VINOD and SUSHMA. They surprise him with their visit.

**KALU:** Wow, wow, wonderful! You guys totally surprised me. Had you informed me I would have come to pick you up at airport.

**SUSHMA:** That is what we never wanted to do. We both had planned to give you a pleasant surprise.

**VINOD:** See the glowing face of my bosom friend. Kalu! See the mirror and you will yourself notice the sudden change.

They laugh and settle in, with SUSHMA taking over the kitchen.

**KALU:** You may be tired of traveling. I have also tried my hands in cooking these days. I'll prepare breakfast and tea for you.

**SUSHMA:** No way! We are not ready to take so much risk.

**VINOD:** (to KALU) Just remain seated. I'll not allow anyone to disobey my wife.

Laughter breaks in.

**INT. KALU'S DINING ROOM - NIGHT**

They enjoy a home-cooked meal, laughing and joking.

**KALU:** Alas, today if Sunanda be here, how nice it would have been!

**SUSHMA:** Oh! It seems you didn't like meals prepared by me.

**KALU:** Sorry, Bhabhi! You have taken it otherwise.

**VINOD:** Never praise any lady in front of another lady. It always creates problems.

**KALU:** (catching his ears and bending) I am ready to be cock like in school days.

Laughter breaks in.

Conversation back to lighter topics.

**INT. DISCO - NIGHT**

VINOD, SUSHMA, and KALU go out to a luxurious hotel on Sushma's insistence. Vinod and Sushma start dancing in the disco. After few minutes Sushma pulls KALU to dance floor and after initial hesitation, he starts dancing. Soon he dances so nicely that it impresses everyone and all start clapping. He feels light and happy.

**INT. DEENDAYAL'S LIVING ROOM - DAY**

DEENDAYAL receives a phone call from his nephew, who saw KALU dancing with a lady. DEENDAYAL scolds him for his complaining tone and defends KALU.

**DEENDAYAL:** How many times you went to look after your Jijaji when he was sulking in deep sorrow after Sunanda's demise? Not a single time. Then why such complaint today if you saw him somewhat relaxing. I am going to advise him to get married again, because it will be very difficult for him to spend the rest of his life alone.

His son KAUSTUBH argues

**KAUSTUBH:** Why are you scolding him? After all Sunanda was also his cousin sister. That's why he felt bad and informed us.

**DEENDAYAL:** And who is Kalika Ji now? After Sunanda's death, our relationship has ended. He is my son in law and as much as dear to me as Sunanda was. Is it not our duty to mitigate his sufferings? You are thinking about her who is no more and not thinking of those who are alive and were so near dear to your sister that her soul will never rest in peace seeing them in agony. Shame on my upbringing if your thinking is so low.

**KAUSTUBH:** Sorry Papa! You are absolutely right. We should do everything possible to get Jijaji out of depression and provide him a happy life, so that Didi can also find peace in that world.

**INT. KALU'S LIVING ROOM - DAY**

VINOD and SUSHMA decide to extend their stay, and they continue to enjoy their time together.

**INT. KALU'S DINING ROOM - DAY**

While having breakfast, they discuss the probable date of engagement between PULKIT and RUCHI within a month or so. KALU entrusts VINOD and SUSHMA with tasks of consulting children and relatives for taking the final decision.

**SUSHMA:** Now don't take tension and enjoy the extended holiday of three days. Brother, you should be relaxed and have refreshments.

**FADE TO BLACK**

**Themes and Notes:**

This chapter focuses on the themes of friendship, healing, and moving forward.

**Friendship and Support:** VINOD and SUSHMA's visit to KALU is a beautiful demonstration of friendship and support. They bring laughter, joy, and a sense of normalcy back into KALU's life.

**Healing and Moving Forward:** KALU's dancing and the overall joyful atmosphere symbolize his healing process. The chapter also introduces the idea of KALU remarrying, showing that life must go on.

**Family Dynamics:** DEENDAYAL's conversation with his nephew and son highlights the importance of family support and understanding. It also emphasizes the ongoing connection to SUNANDA, even after her death.

**Character Development:** KALU's character continues to grow as he begins to find joy again. VINOD and SUSHMA's playful and caring personalities shine through, and DEENDAYAL's wisdom and compassion are evident.

**Visual and Symbolic Elements:** The dancing scene is a visual representation of KALU's return to life and joy. The home-cooked meals symbolize comfort, connection, and healing.

**Tone and Mood:** The tone is light and joyful, with moments of humor and warmth. There's a sense of hope and renewal, tempered by the underlying grief.

**Dialogue and Interaction:** The dialogue is playful and authentic, reflecting the close relationship between the characters. The banter and teasing add to the lively atmosphere.

This screenplay offers a heartwarming exploration of friendship, healing, and moving forward. The characters' interactions and the visual elements create a rich and engaging narrative that resonates with themes of love, loss, and renewal.

# Scene 35

**INT. KALU'S LIVING ROOM - NIGHT**

Camera panning from outside of Kalu's house moving in to living room and covering Vinod, Sushma and Kalu focuses on Sushma.

VINOD, SUSHMA, and KALU are chatting after dinner. SUSHMA becomes emotional, expressing her concern for KALU's loneliness.

**SUSHMA:** Elder brother! We have lived every moment of the last nine days in a wonderful way and to be honest, it has been the best experience of my life. Tomorrow we have to go and from now on we are apprehensive about you again…

**KALU:** No, no! I will try my best that the hard work done by both of you for nine days does not go in vain.

VINOD hesitantly suggests that KALU consider remarrying. KALU remains silent, and they avoid further discussion.

**INT. HYDERABAD AIRPORT - MORNING**

KALU drops VINOD and SUSHMA off at the airport and unexpectedly runs into his father-in-law DEENDAYAL and brother-in-law KAUSTUBH.

**DEENDAYAL:** How did you know that we are coming?

**KALU:** No, I was having no idea about your arrival. I have come to drop off my friend when suddenly I saw you. You should have informed me but anyway it's good to find you here. Let's drive to comfort of home where we can have further chit-chat along with breakfast and tea.

They head towards KALU's home.

**INT. KALU'S LIVING ROOM - EVENING**

DEENDAYAL, KAUSTUBH, and KALU are sipping tea. DEENDAYAL brings up the subject of remarriage.

**DEENDAYAL:** Engineer sir, we have to talk to you about something special, if you don't mind. You are humbly requested to think seriously about second marriage.

**KALU:** So kind of you. You are too good natured to suggest it . But people are not so generous. Today, if I accept your advice, then most of the people in the society will come forward to slander me and question the mutual attachment between me and Sunanda.

They discuss the matter at length, with DEENDAYAL and KAUSTUBH urging KALU to consider their proposal.

**KAUSTUBH:** Take your time according to your convenience and then take the right decision after thinking carefully.

### INT. KALU'S LIVING ROOM - VARIOUS DAYS

Montage of KALU spending quality time with DEENDAYAL and KAUSTUBH over the next three days. They visit SHREYA's in-laws, discuss wedding plans for PULKIT and RUCHI, and enjoy each other's company. The discussion of remarriage surfaces off and on but Kalu remains non-comittal.

### INT. HYDERABAD AIRPORT - DAY

KALU sees DEENDAYAL and KAUSTUBH off, promising to consider their proposal.

### INT. KALU'S LIVING ROOM - NIGHT

KALU reflects on his situation, struggling with the idea of remarriage and the loneliness he will have to face lifelong.

**KALU: (V.O.)** They are genuine in their suggestions. But how can I forget her and start living with another woman. I know it will be tough to remain alone particularly when I fell ill. Who will take care if I have a sudden fall or sudden loss of consciousness. Loneliness may disturb my mental balance too. Overall, destiny has put me in a confused state.

Unable to sleep, he reads a magazine and eventually falls asleep on the sofa.

**FADE TO BLACK**

**Themes and Notes:**

**Moving On:** The central theme of this chapter is the challenge of moving on after a significant loss. KALU's friends and family recognize his loneliness and encourage him to consider remarriage, but he struggles with societal judgments and his loyalty to SUNANDA.

**Family Support:** DEENDAYAL and KAUSTUBH's visit emphasizes the importance of family support. They approach the subject of remarriage with sensitivity and understanding, recognizing KALU's needs and concerns.

**Societal Pressures:** KALU's hesitation to remarry is influenced by societal judgments and the fear of being slandered. This highlights the societal pressures that can affect personal decisions.

**Character Development:** KALU's character continues to evolve as he grapples with his emotions and the idea of moving forward. DEENDAYAL and KAUSTUBH's characters are portrayed as compassionate and wise.

**Visual and Symbolic Elements:** The visual contrast between the lively atmosphere during the visits of friends and family and KALU's solitude when alone symbolizes his internal struggle.

**Tone and Mood:** The tone is thoughtful and introspective, with moments of warmth and connection balanced by KALU's internal turmoil.

**Dialogue and Interaction:** The dialogue is heartfelt and genuine, reflecting the deep connections between the characters. The discussions about remarriage are handled with care and respect.

This screenplay offers a nuanced exploration of grief, healing, and the complexities of moving on. The interactions between KALU and his family provide insight into the emotional challenges he faces, and the visual elements create a rich and engaging narrative that resonates with themes of love, loss, and renewal.

# Scene 36

**INT. RUCHI'S HOSTEL'S VISITORS ROOM - DAY**

Camera panning over from Girls hostel board to cover outside of building and moves in to visitor's room, then focuses on Pulkit talking on phone.

VINOD is on the phone with RUCHI and PULKIT, discussing the engagement date and expressing concern about KALU's loneliness.

**VINOD:** (to Pulkit) Son! If not for marriage, at least fix some date for engagement. We had a discussion with your father and he has entrusted me with the responsibility of talking to you.

**PULKIT:** Ok, uncle! Ruchi and I have discussed about it. Any Saturday or Sunday of next month which is December will be fine for us. Rest you guardians decide and inform us.

But I want to seek your advice regarding some thing very special as Papa's closest friend. Me and Ruchi have come to the conclusion that the best remedy for his loneliness will be his remarriage as we can't leave him suffering alone. You must also be worried about him.

**VINOD:** That's like a worthy son! Me and Sushma have been at Hyderabad with him for nine days and found him in very bad shape. Actually we tried to discuss with him about remarriage but he didn't open up keeping mum. You children can do better.

They agree on a plan to consider a second marriage for KALU and implement it during engagement.

**PULKIT:** But uncle! First of all we have to search for a widow or divorcee.

**VINOD:** To me, one potential option in sight but you will have to talk to Makalu and make him ready to discuss it with his mother.

**PULKIT:** Uncle! You are genius. What a perfect choice! Monka aunty so close to my papa and mummy that she can be easily made ready for the proposal with help of Makalu. I will talk to him after consulting Shreya didi and Siddhi Jiju.

**VINOD:** Go ahead. I'll try to take Chanda's help.

**INT. VINOD'S STUDY - DAY**

VINOD talks to CHANDA about the idea of KALU's remarriage.

**VINOD:** From the condition of Kalu we saw in Hyderabad, it is not safe to leave him alone.

**CHANDA:** I also consider him my closest friend, and actually should have taken initiative. I will try my best. I'll talk to Monika and Kalu to grab this second opportunity, life has provided them to get back their first love. Now It is our duty to somehow implement this plan.

**INT. SHREYA'S LIVING ROOM - DAY**

PULKIT and SHREYA are on the phone with MAKALU, discussing the idea of bringing KALU and MONIKA together.

**PULKIT :** (on phone to Makalu) Hi dear Makalu! Shreya didi is also on line. Do you remember us.

**MAKALU:** How can I forget such nice friends like you. Me and Mumma always remember you all and were in profound grief hearing about aunty's demise. Now uncle would be too lonely. I have seen mumma's suffering, passing life alone after divorce and now uncle landed in same precarious situation.

**SHREYA:** Exactly! We want to discuss a solution regarding this if you don't mind.

**MAKALU:** I don't believe in formalities among friends. You can talk straight forward.

**PULKIT:** We have an idea of remarriage between Papa and your Mumma to bring them together out of their wilderness.

**MAKALU:** Beautiful idea! I really liked it. Give me some time. I will definitely convince my mother for this, I am sure.

They agree to work together on the plan.

**INT. KALU'S LIVING ROOM - DAY**

VINOD talks to KALU about the engagement date, and they finalize the details.

**VINOD:** The children have agreed for the engagement on any Saturday or Sunday of December, but they will marry only after six months.

**KALU:** Last Sunday afternoon of December will be fine as it will be easy for all to take leave around Christmas.

**VINOD:** Good suggestion! Make it final to be solemnised at some good hotel at Patna.

**KALU:** Done.

### INT. MAKALU'S LIVING ROOM - NIGHT

MAKALU talks to MONIKA on phone about the idea of moving back to India and spending time with KALU.

**MAKALU:** Altering our plan to Europe, we should make trip to India. We will stay with Kalu uncle for ten days before going anywhere else as he is so alone there after aunty's death. Atleast we can try to mitigate his sufferings to some extent.

**MONIKA:** Agreed. You have grown up now.

**MAKALU:** Let me finish. I think you should consider the option of settling back in India as you feel better there among your friends.

**MONIKA:** My Makalu has become very smart and has started worrying a lot about mumma. I will definitely consider your advice.

**INT. KALU'S LIVING ROOM - NIGHT**

MONIKA is on the phone with KALU, discussing their visit to Hyderabad.

**MONIKA:** Me and Makalu will spend ten days with you at your residence in Hyderabad, if you don't mind. This has been suggested by Makalu.

**KALU:** What are you talking about? Why at all will I start to mind? On the contrary, I would be very happy.

**MONIKA:** Look, whether it'll tarnish your clean image or not.

**KALU:** (laughing) Now, I am not so coward.

**MAKALU:** I am coming to test myself your boldness.

They tease each other and share a laugh.

### FADE TO BLACK

**Themes and Notes:**

**Concern for Kalu:** The central theme of this chapter is the growing concern for KALU's loneliness and the collaborative effort to find a solution.

**Planning for Second Marriage:** Various family members and friends work together to explore the idea of a second marriage for KALU, considering MONIKA as a potential partner.

**Family Support:** The chapter emphasizes the importance of family support and collaboration, with everyone working together to ensure KALU's well-being.

**Character Development:** Characters like VINOD, CHANDA, PULKIT, SHREYA, MAKALU, and MONIKA play significant roles in this chapter, showcasing their concern, empathy, and determination.

**Visual and Symbolic Elements:** The visual elements include various settings where the characters discuss and plan, reflecting their interconnected relationships.

**Dialogue and Interaction:** The dialogue is heartfelt and purposeful, with characters expressing their concerns and working together to find a solution.

**Tone and Mood:** The tone is hopeful and collaborative, with moments of humor and warmth.

This screenplay offers a rich exploration of family dynamics, friendship, and the complexities of moving on after a loss. The interactions between the characters provide insight into their relationships and shared goals, and the visual elements create a cohesive narrative that resonates with themes of love, support, and renewal.

# Scene 37

**INT. KALU'S BEDROOM - NIGHT**

Camera opens up panning over Kalu's house moving in to his bedroom and focuses on Kalu lying on bed.

Kalu is lying on the bed, lost in thought, reflecting on life and the possibility of a second marriage.

**KALU** (V.O.): Life looks like a game of snakes and ladders. Sometimes you are nearing goal of complete satisfaction but some tragedy bites like snake and you fall back to floor just like after Sunanda left me alone. Now, people are talking about remarriage as if providing me ladder to come out of hole. If I really want to remarry, who can be better than Monika but will she be ready to settle back in India. Will my kids like it or not? Should Makalu accept me or not? Perhaps the final decision will have to wait for the answer from time.

**INT. MONIKA'S BEDROOM - NIGHT**

MONIKA is also struggling with similar questions, reflecting on her past and future.

**MONIKA** (V.O.): I am an advocate and I can very well understand what Makalu wanted to say. But Kalu is not same unmarried young bloke. Now he has a past and will compare with Sunanda. Will she be able to prepare herself to bear that comparison? Will Makalu, Shreya, and Pulkit be able to reconcile with each other?

She receives a call from NEHAL, who jokingly proposes to her.

**NEHAL:** If you have any plan to come back to India, I will like you to work in my legal firm as I get little time as home minister of Maharashtra to look after.

**MONIKA:** Hi! Thanks for call and the offer. But I have good legal practice here and Makalu is running a coffee shop at Toronto, Canada. So better hand it over to your wife or children.

**NEHAL:** I remain unmarried. Now, if you say, I will marry you today. Sorry if you didn't like the joke.

**MONIKA:** But who gave you my number?

**NEHAL:** How it matters? Now I can talk to my old friend off and on.

Phone rings again after some time. Chanda this time.

**CHANDA:** How are you, dear!

**MONIKA:** Fine. What a coincidence that all old friends are calling today. Just now Nehal has phoned to propose for job in his firm alongwith marriage free. Ha ha ha!

**CHANDA:** What? From where he got your number?

**MONIKA:** I don't know.

**CHANDA:** Engagement of Ruchi and Pulkit has been scheduled on last Sunday of December at Patna. You plan to be there without any excuse.

**MONIKA:** Well! I have already planned to come with Makalu and will first go to Hyderabad to stay with Kalu for ten days before going anywhere.

**CHANDA:** That sounds good. Why not you think about encasing this second opportunity to unite with your first love. It'll be good for both of you.

**MONIKA:** You too, Chanda! Let time decide it. Whether children on either side will like it or not? It's also a big question.

**CHANDA:** Actually it's their proposal. You both take your time to decide.

MONIKA is left pondering the situation.

**INT. VINOD'S LIVING ROOM - DAY**

Chanda confronts Vinod about sharing information with Nehal.

**CHANDA:** Till now, he used to roam freely as a bachelor and had completely forgotten Monika. Hearing about the marriage prospects of Kalu and Monika, crackers of marriage started bursting in his mind.

Vinod apologizes, and they make a plan to keep Nehal away from MONIKA.

**CHANDA:** We have to work twice as hard. At the time of engagement, Nehal will not be allowed to get close to Monika. We will surely succeed.

**INT. JEWELRY STORE - DAY**

Chanda and SUSHMA are choosing rings for the engagement.

**SUSHMA:** For whom did you choose the second pair of rings, asking to keep them safe?

Chanda avoids the question, and they continue shopping.

**INT. SHREYA AND SIDDHI'S LIVING ROOM - DAY**

Shreya, Siddhi, Ruchi, and Pulkit discuss preparations for the engagement and decide to call Kalu to Mumbai for shopping.

**RUCHI:** The whole family will also market together and while having fun together, we will also decide the finer points of the preparation for the engagement.

They call Kalu and convince him to come to Mumbai this Friday.

**FADE TO BLACK**

**Themes and Notes:**

**Contemplation and Decision Making:** The chapter focuses on the contemplation and decision-making process of Kalu and Monika regarding the possibility of a second marriage. Both characters are shown to be struggling with complex emotions and questions.

**Interference and Planning:** The interference of Nehal adds a twist to the story, leading to strategic planning by Vinod and Chanda to keep him away from Monika.

**Family Dynamics:** The chapter also explores the dynamics between various family members as they prepare for the engagement, showcasing their relationships and interactions.

**Character Development:** Characters like Kalu, Monika, Vinod, Chanda, Nehal, Shreya, Siddhi, Ruchi, and Pulkit play significant roles in this chapter, each contributing to the unfolding narrative.

**Visual and Symbolic Elements:** The visual elements include various settings where the characters discuss, shop, and plan, reflecting their interconnected relationships.

**Dialogue and Interaction:** The dialogue is rich and purposeful, with characters expressing their thoughts, concerns, and intentions.

**Tone and Mood:** The tone is contemplative and strategic, with moments of humor, tension, and warmth.

This screenplay offers a nuanced exploration of love, decision-making, family dynamics, and strategic planning. The interactions between the characters provide insight into their relationships and shared goals, and the visual elements create a cohesive narrative that resonates with themes of love, support, and renewal. The chapter sets the stage for further developments in the story, building anticipation for what lies ahead.

❑❑

# Scene 38

**INT. HYDERABAD AIRPORT - DAY**

Camera panning over the airport, moving to arrival exit gate focuses on Monika and Makalu.

Monika and Makalu greet Kalu as he arrives.

**MAKALU:** (waving his right hand) Hello Kalika uncle! I'm Makalu. This way.

Coming close to him, touhes his feet. After showering blessings Kalu hugs him.

**KALU:** Long live, my child! Nice parenting, Monika!

**MAKALU:** Thanks, uncle. Can I call you Daddy as you called me your child.

**KALU:** Yes, if your mumma has no problem.

**MONIKA:** No problem. Call each other the way you like.

Kalu is impressed by Makalu's manners and the bond between two starts developing stronger.

**INT. KALU'S HOUSE - NIGHT**

Kalu is asleep, tears on his pillow. Monika sleeping in next room rises hearing sound of sobbing. After few moments of hesitation tries to knock the door of Kalu's room but it opens up on putting hand. She enters, concerned.

**MONIKA:** (softly) "Kalu?"

But he is in deep slumber.

She finds pillow wet on either side of his head with tears rolling down.

Out of emotion she puts his head in her lap slowly running fingers through his hairs. Kalu wakes up and slowly raises eyelids looking directly into her eyes.

They share an emotional moment, confessing their love for each other.

**KALU:** Look, life has given us another chance. So, I am confessing my love as promised, before you. If you accept….

Monika kisses him, sealing her confession.

**MONIKA:** I will never ask you to forget Sunanda. If you don't want to marry we can live in as in America.

**KALU:** Relax! As we have crossed the boundary, all obstacles will be removed now. Wait for approval from seniors and children and everything will be resolved.

**INT. 'JEWEL OF NIZAM - THE MINAR' TOWER RESTAURANT - DAY**

Kalu, Monika, and Makalu enjoy a lavish meal, bonding over food and conversation.

**MAKALU:** Daddy, thank you very much for this wonderful feast served in silver utensils like royal family. You have changed the meaning of the word 'father' for me. I have impression of a tight lipped serious admonishing never smiling person as father. You are so loving and caring father that I feel jealous of Shreya di and Pulkit bhaiya.

Kalu reassures Makalu, promising love and support equal to them.

**INT. HOTEL - NIGHT**

Guests arrive for the engagement party. Vinod and Chanda arrange a suit with double rooms for Kalu, Monika, and Makalu, ensuring complete privacy.

**INT. HOTEL ROOM - NIGHT**

Vinod, Chanda, Shreya, Siddhi, Makalu, and Pulkit urge Kalu and Monika to get married.

**RUCHI:** Let's decide before our engagement tomorrow, so that both of you can be engaged along with us.

Elders including Daya Babu, Deen Dayal Ji, Mr Ganeshan, Mrs Jayanthi and Mahanand Babu join in and heeding to their request Kalu and Monika agree to the proposal. Two touch feet of elders one by one and get their blessings.

**INT. HOTEL DINING ROOM - MORNING**

Guests gather for Breakfast. All family members are also having it.

Nehal arrives, expressing interest in Monika and her return to India.

**NEHAL:** What's the matter? We have met after so many years, you seem completely changed. What about my advocacy business proposal?

**MONIKA:** If you think of shifting your office to Hyderabad, I can consider.

MONIKA plays along, leaving Nehal intrigued.

**FADE TO BLACK**

**Themes and Notes:**

**Emotional Connection:** The chapter focuses on the deep emotional connection between Kalu and Monika, culminating in their confession of love.

**Family Bonding:** The interactions between Kalu, Monika, Makalu, and other family members highlight the importance of family bonds and shared values.

**Strategic Planning:** The arrangements made by Vinod, Chanda, and others for the engagement party, as well as the push for Kalu and Monika's marriage, demonstrate careful planning and collaboration.

**Cultural Appreciation:** The visit to the 'Jewel of Nizam - The Minar' tower restaurant showcases a rich appreciation for Hyderabadi civilization and culinary traditions.

**Character Development:** Characters like Kalu, Monika, Makalu, Nehal, Vinod, Chanda, Shreya, Siddhi, Pulkit, and Ruchi play significant roles, each contributing to the unfolding narrative.

**Visual and Symbolic Elements:** The visual elements include various settings such as the airport, Kalu's house, the tower restaurant, and the hotel, reflecting the characters' interconnected relationships.

**Dialogue and Interaction:** The dialogue is rich and purposeful, with characters expressing their thoughts, concerns, intentions, and emotions.

**Tone and Mood:** The tone is warm and affectionate, with moments of tension, intrigue, and celebration.

**Conflict and Intrigue:** Nehal's presence adds an element of intrigue and potential conflict, setting the stage for further developments.

This screenplay offers a heartfelt exploration of love, family, strategic planning, and cultural appreciation. The interactions between the characters provide insight into their relationships, shared goals, and emotional connections. The visual elements create a cohesive narrative that resonates with themes of love, support, and renewal. The chapter sets the stage for further developments in the story, building anticipation for what lies ahead.

❏❏

# Scene 39

**INT. HOTEL ROOM - DAY**

Camera panning from outside of hotel moves in to Nehal's room and focuses on Nehal pacing to and fro.

Nehal, restless and after a while appears determined. He comes out to hotel lobby, tries to locate Monika. He's driven by love and desperation.

**NEHAL:** (to himself) I must find her. I must tell her how I feel.

He roams here and there but meets no success as Monika has left for the market, when he reaches her room to find Makalu alone there, not recognising him and divulging her whereabouts.

**INT. HOTEL AUDITORIUM - DAY**

Guests gather for the engagement ceremony. Nehal takes his seat, eyes scanning for Monika.

**INT. BACKSTAGE - DAY**

Nehal approaches Monika, but Shreya intervenes as planned before.

**SHREYA:** Aunty, please see my dance steps. Your guidance is very important.

Nehal, frustrated, returns to his seat.

**INT. HOTEL AUDITORIUM - DAY**

The dance and music performances begin. Family members perform, building excitement and joy.

**INT. HOTEL AUDITORIUM - STAGE - DAY**

Pulkit proposes to Ruchi, but she sets a condition.

**RUCHI:** I accept your love, but Monika Aunty and Kalika Uncle must get engaged first.

The crowd agrees and start chanting their names in chorus.

Kalu and Monika are brought on stage. They exchange rings, followed by Pulkit and Ruchi.

### INT. HOTEL DINING AREA - DAY

Nehal, defeated, attempts to leave but is stopped by Makalu, Kalu, Vinod, Chanda, and Monika.

**KALU:** Please stay for lunch, my friend.

Nehal reluctantly agrees, offering congratulations and best wishes.

### INT. HOTEL ROOM - EVENING

Close friends and family gather to discuss the wedding date, settling on a date in May.

**MONIKA:** I'll like to stay with Babuji Daya Prasad ji at our home in Patna for a week before returning to America.

**KALU:** of course, but I will also like to visit your home and take blessings from your family members. We will stay there for atleast two days and I will try to gel with them.

Everyone is pleased with the arrangements.

**INT. DAYA BABU'S HOUSE – DAY**

Daya Babu enjoys the company of Kalu, Monika, and Makalu, finding joy in their presence.

**DAYA BABU:** (to Makalu) Tell me more about America, my boy.

They chat and bond, bringing happiness to Daya Babu's life.

**FADE TO BLACK**

**Themes and Notes:**

**Love and Desperation:** Nehal's desperation to express his love for Monika drives his actions, but he's thwarted by fate and the plans of others.

**Family Celebration:** The engagement ceremony is a joyful occasion, filled with music, dance, and love. The performances by family members add to the festive atmosphere.

**Destiny and Acceptance:** Nehal's acceptance of his fate, though painful, underscores the theme of destiny. He recognizes that he has lost Monika and vows to remain celibate.

**Planning and Unity:** The family's collaboration in planning the wedding date and Monika's decision to stay with Daya Babu reflect their unity and shared goals.

**Character Development:** Characters like Nehal, Kalu, Monika, Pulkit, Ruchi, Shreya, Makalu, and others continue to evolve, each playing a role in the unfolding narrative.

**Visual and Symbolic Elements:** The visual elements include the hotel auditorium, the engagement stage, the dining area, and Daya Babu's house. The engagement rings symbolize commitment and love.

**Dialogue and Interaction:** The dialogue is rich with emotion, intention, and character dynamics. The interactions between characters reveal their relationships, desires, and decisions.

**Tone and Mood:** The tone is celebratory and joyful, with moments of tension, frustration, and acceptance.

**Conflict and Resolution:** The conflict between Nehal's desire and the family's plans is resolved through acceptance and the fulfillment of the engagements.

This screenplay captures the joy of family celebration, the pain of unrequited love, and the satisfaction of planning for the future. The interactions between characters provide insight into their relationships and emotions, while the visual elements create a cohesive and engaging narrative. The chapter concludes with a sense of contentment and anticipation, setting the stage for the next phase of the characters' lives.

❑❑

# Scene 40

**INT. DELHI AIRPORT - DAY**

Camera opens up panning over outside the Departure gate and focuses on Kalu, Monika and Makalu.

Kalu, Monika, and Makalu prepare to say goodbye.

**KALU:** (to Makalu) Take care of yourself, son. Your coming and being with me really helped a lot.

**MAKALU:** Daddy, I am lucky to have you. Make a plan to visit Canada and the US soon.

Nehal unexpectedly appears.

**NEHAL:** (approaching) Hi, guys! What a happy coincidence, you guys are here.

## INT. DELHI AIRPORT - CONTINUOUS

Nehal apologizes for his behavior during the engagement. Kalu and Monika forgive him.

**NEHAL:** I wanted to apologize to both of you for my bad behavior. I lost my temper.

**KALU:** It happens, friend. Any one in place of you would have done that.

(To Monika) He is your silent lover and remained unmarried because of that love. If he would have got the chance, he could have flied to America to marry you but he never told you about his love.

**NEHAL:** No, no! It's not true. When I learnt from Vinod about possibility of remarriage between you two, I not only disapproved it but even tried to propose Monika under the cover of joke. I am too mean and selfish. Not worthy of being called your friend. But you two have got large hearts and can forgive my unpardonable act.

**KALU:** You were our good friend and will always be.

**MONIKA:** I request you to forget this failed love and find a life partner for yourself.

**NEHAL:** (pleading) If you have really forgiven me, then do think about taking over my business.

**KALU:** Stop unnecessarily blaming yourself and free your soul from this burden of sin.

They say their goodbyes, and Monika, Makalu, and Nehal enter the airport.

**INT. FOREIGN DEPARTMENT OFFICE - DAY**

Kalu meets a friend to discuss Monika's options for returning to India permanently.

**FRIEND:** She should get the card by applying for 'Overseas Citizen of India'. She will be exempted from the condition of going again and again to America to keep citizenship intact.

**KALU:** Thank you very much for giving the best solution to my problem.

**INT. MONIKA'S MANSION - AMERICA - DAY**

Kalu arrives in America and is impressed by Monika's grand mansion and lifestyle.

**INT. VARIOUS LOCATIONS - AMERICA - DAY**

Monika takes Kalu on a two-week tour of beautiful romantic cities.

**KALU:** (revealing his doubts) How appropriate would it be for you to return to India permanently?

**MONIKA:** (reprimanding) Amman yaar, what soil are you made of? I will sell it all and leave. I want to live a comfortable life just wrapped in your arms.

**KALU:** I don't know when will I get rid of the habit of spoiling the happiness.

**MONIKA:** Don't worry, my Devdas! Chandramukhi has come in your life, to remove Paro's deficiency.

They laugh together, embracing their new beginning.

**FADE TO BLACK**

**Themes and Notes:**

**Forgiveness and Redemption:** Nehal's heartfelt apology and Kalu and Monika's forgiveness highlight the theme of redemption. Nehal's willingness to expose his faults and seek forgiveness demonstrates his sincerity.

**Love and Commitment:** Kalu and Monika's relationship deepens as they prepare for their future together. Their interactions reflect their love, understanding, and commitment to each other.

**Transition and New Beginnings:** The chapter marks a transition as Monika and Makalu prepare to return to America, and Kalu makes arrangements for Monika's permanent return to India. The tour of America symbolizes their new beginning.

**Character Development:** Characters like Kalu, Monika, Makalu, and Nehal continue to evolve. Their interactions reveal their emotions, intentions, and relationships.

**Visual and Symbolic Elements:** The visual elements include the Delhi airport, the Foreign Department office, Monika's mansion, and various romantic locations in America. The Overseas Citizen of India card symbolizes Monika's connection to India.

**Dialogue and Interaction:** The dialogue is rich with emotion, intention, and character dynamics. The interactions between characters reveal their relationships, desires, and decisions.

**Tone and Mood:** The tone is reflective and hopeful, with moments of tension, forgiveness, romance, and joy.

**Conflict and Resolution:** The conflict between Nehal's guilt and Kalu and Monika's forgiveness is resolved through understanding and compassion. The conflict between Kalu's doubts and Monika's determination is resolved through communication and commitment.

This screenplay captures the complexities of love, forgiveness, and transition. The interactions between characters provide insight into their relationships and emotions, while the visual elements create a cohesive and engaging narrative. The chapter concludes with a sense of hope and anticipation, setting the stage for Kalu and Monica's new life together.

❑❑

# Scene 41

**INT. WEDDING VENUE - NIGHT**

Camera opens up panning over wedding venue moves towards mandap capturing Monika and Kalu taking wedding rounds.

Priests chant marriage spells in Sanskrit and Hindi.

Nehal watches as Monika and Kalu take their wedding rounds. The joyous occasion is filled with laughter, love, and celebration.

**NEHAL:** (V.O.) Today I am not feeling anything bad about Monika and Kalu tying wedding knot and rejoicing in seeing the desolate world of my beloved getting settled. I am seeking my happiness in her happy future. Probably with all hope of reunion gone into the wind, I am changed man now.

Monika enjoying all marriage rituals with full enthusiasm while Kalu time and again reminisces into past, scenes of his first marriage with Sunanda passing in front of his eyes, though unwillingly. He is trying his best to hide his mixed feelings particularly from Monika.

**INT. WEDDING VENUE - RECEPTION - NEXT NIGHT**

Monika and Kalu celebrate with family and friends as Ruchi and Pulkit getting married with much fanfare at the same venue. Monika enjoying the role of bridegroom's mother very much without feeling awkward of herself being married yesterday night. Pulkit and Ruchi also giving her proper respect during every ritual.

**INT. KALU'S HOUSE - DAY**

Monika seamlessly integrates into the family, winning everyone's heart.

## INT. KALU'S HOUSE - NIGHT - 2 DAYS LATER

Kalu and Monika discuss honeymoon plans for Ruchi and Pulkit.

**KALU:** Where would it be appropriate to send Ruchi and Pulkit for their honeymoon? I'll have to arrange for the same to send them next week.

**MONIKA:** You are always late. I have made all the arrangements. They will leave day after tomorrow to Switzerland and will also cover two nearby countries in fifteen days. They wanted to go to Toronto as promised to Makalu but I convinced them to begin their love life at the most beautiful places of world and Canada can be visted later.

**KALU:** (romantically) What have you thought for ourselves, sweetheart?

Where do you intend to show the flames of your beauty?

**MONIKA:** (playfully) We don't need to compete with young couple. We will conserve our energy without wasting it in roaming around and use it here in mutual wrestling. What else is needed in honeymoon other than me, you and none around! If we want to play long inning well, will have to conserve passion and stamina.

**KALU:** I take it without sarcastic note on me only. So it's final we are staying at Hyderabad and going nowhere. Other day, you don't start calling me miser.

**MONIKA:** (smiling) That I will definitely do as fundamental right of wife.

**INT. KALU'S HOUSE - DAY**

Ruchi and Pulkit express their displeasure knowing that parents are not accompanying them on the honeymoon.

**MONIKA:** Now you are mature adults. You are no more required to hold our fingers to go anywhere. Neither we will interfere in your conjugal life nor allow you to do so in our and this rule is effective with immediate effect.

**PULKIT and RUCHI:** Mummy! You are great. Left no space for us to utter a single word.

**RUCHI:** But we request you people also to visit somewhere.

**KALU:** We are also grown adults, enough to decide for ourselves.

**RUCHI:** See the harmony between two. We should learn from them.

They all laugh together.

**INT. KALU'S HOUSE - DAY - WEEK LATER**

Monika persuades Kalu to return to the office after a week of honeymoon at home.

**MONIKA:** We will soon get bored if this honeymoon continues longer. That's why you start doing daytime entertainment in the office. The night program will continue as before.

**KALU:** But you will be absolutely bored in my absence. How will you pass your time? Come with me to my office.

**MONIKA:** (mimicking) Come with me. Looks like going to romance in the garden, not the office. Neither you will work there nor your colleagues, all will keep on staring at my beautiful face. I'll lose some weight here while waiting for you and become slim.

## FADE TO BLACK

**Themes and Notes:**

**New Beginnings:** The chapter marks the beginning of new chapters in the lives of the characters. Monika and Kalu's wedding, Ruchi and Pulkit's marriage, and the integration of Monika into the family symbolize new beginnings.

**Love and Acceptance:** The love and acceptance between the characters are evident in their interactions. Nehal's acceptance of Monika's happiness, Kalu and Monka's playful romance, and the family's joyous celebration reflect the theme of love and acceptance.

**Aging and Wisdom:** The contrast between the young couple's aspirations and the seasoned couple's wisdom highlights the differences in perspective that come with age. The young couple dreams of a fantasy life, while the older couple anticipates problems and plans for the future.

**Character Development:** The characters continue to evolve, with Monika seamlessly integrating into the family, Kalu balancing his past and present, and Nehal finding peace in his love for Monika.

**Visual and Symbolic Elements:** The visual elements include the wedding venue, Kalu's house, and the playful interactions between the characters. The weddings symbolize new beginnings, while the discussions about honeymoons reflect the characters' perspectives on love and life.

**Dialogue and Interaction:** The dialogue is filled with humor, love, and wisdom. The interactions between the characters reveal their relationships, emotions, and intentions.

**Tone and Mood:** The tone is joyful and reflective, with moments of humor, love, and acceptance.

**Conflict and Resolution:** The conflicts in this chapter are minor and resolved through communication and understanding. The discussions about honeymoons and Kalu's return to the office are resolved through playful banter and mutual agreement.

This screenplay captures the joyous celebration of new beginnings, the dynamics of love and acceptance, and the wisdom that comes with age. The interactions between the characters provide insight into their relationships and emotions, while the visual elements create a cohesive and engaging narrative. The chapter concludes with a sense of contentment and anticipation, setting the stage for the characters' new lives together.

❑❑

# Scene 42

**INT. KALU'S LIVING ROOM - EVENING**

Camera panning living room focuses on to Monika's angry looking face.

Monika expresses her frustration at being a housewife, comparing love to the thirst for water and how it changes over time.

**MONIKA:** It's been three years since I got married and living the routine of a simple housewife... All that remains the aim of my life is to keep searching for my happiness in my husband's happiness.

Kalu is shocked at Monika's sudden outburst.

**KALU:** What happened, sweetheart? When I went in the morning, everything was fine. But you have decided to stay at home and adopted role of house wife at your will.

**MONIKA:** (angrily) How selfish you men are! If I wanted to take that decision in the spirit of sacrifice for you, why did not you stop me?

**KALU:** I accept my fault and you have every right to reprimand me for my selfish behaviour. You came here to live with me sacrificing all your wealth and luxury alongwith profession and in return I gave you boring long day, confined inside home, only waiting for my return from the office. My love proved much inferior to your. But pardon me for the same.

Suddenly Monika's anger turns into laughter as she reveals it's only a prank to test him.

**MONIKA:** (teasingly) Ha ha ha, what a timid cat my tiger looking lover has turned into! Looks like he will cry very next moment.

Kalu is relieved but warns Monika not to make such serious jokes.

**MONIKA:** (laughing) I can't help you by relinquishing wife's right to quarrel with husband. It really gives immense pleasure to women.

**INT. KALU'S LIVING ROOM - DAY - NEXT DAY**

Kalu brings an application from the Bar Council for Monika to start practicing law again.

**MONIKA:** You took yesterday's incident unnecessarily seriously. There was no need for this.

**KALU:** Just to help the poor and helpless, you should register yourself in the Bar Council as soon as possible and start practicing.

Monika reveals that she's going to be a grandmother, and they celebrate the news.

**INT. PATNA - DAY - WEEKS LATER**

The family gathers for Ruchi's baby shower ceremony. There's joy, laughter, and a sense of unity among the family members.

**INT. PATNA - HOSPITAL - DAY - MONTHS LATER**

Ruchi gives birth to a baby boy, and the family gathers again to celebrate the new addition.

**INT. PATNA - LIVING ROOM - DAY - CHHATHI PUJAN**

Makalu meets his nephew and suggests the name 'Puru' for the child, receiving praise from the family.

## FADE TO BLACK

**Themes and Notes:**

**Love and Marriage:** The chapter explores the dynamics of love and marriage, showing how feelings can change over time. Monika's outburst and subsequent teasing reveal the complexities of their relationship.

**Family Expansion and Joy:** The birth of a new child brings joy and unity to the family. The baby shower and naming ceremony symbolize the expansion of the family and the strengthening of bonds.

**Self-Realization and Growth:** Kalu's gesture to encourage Monika to practice law again shows his understanding of her needs and desires. It reflects growth in their relationship and a willingness to support each other's individuality.

**Visual and Symbolic Elements:** The visual elements include the living room, the baby shower ceremony, the hospital, and the family gatherings. The birth of the child symbolizes new beginnings and the continuation of the family legacy.

**Dialogue and Interaction:** The dialogue is filled with emotion, humor, and love. The interactions between the characters reveal their relationships, feelings, and intentions.

**Tone and Mood:** The tone is joyful and reflective, with moments of tension, humor, and celebration.

**Conflict and Resolution:** The conflicts in this chapter are minor and resolved through communication, understanding, and humor. Monika's outburst is revealed to be a test, and Kalu's gesture to encourage her to practice law shows his support.

**Character Development:** The characters continue to evolve, with Monika expressing her feelings, Kalu showing support, and the family celebrating the new addition.

This screenplay captures the complexities of love and marriage, the joy of family expansion, and the growth and understanding between the characters. The visual elements create a cohesive and engaging narrative, while the dialogue and interactions provide insight into the characters' emotions and relationships. The chapter concludes with a sense of contentment and anticipation, as the family celebrates the new addition and looks forward to the future.

❏❏

# Scene 43

**INT. MONIKA'S LAW OFFICE CHAMBER - DAY (2 YEARS LATER)**

Camera panning over court moves to advocate chamber focussing on Monika.

Monika is frustrated with the lack of clients and the unethical practices of other lawyers. She's approached by various brokers and lawyers who offer empty promises and unsolicited advice.

**LAWYER 1:** Madam, it is just a matter of a few days, you will turn all the senior lawyers jobless. No one is as capable as you. They all do settings to establish their practice.

**LAWYER 2:** Chadda sahib has said absolutely right. All the senior lawyers were not tired of praising you after you got the dismissal of pickpocketting charges on the poor lad in the very first hearing by your strong argument. His case had been lingering for years.

**LAWYER 3**: Very True Akhtar Miyan! If madam compromises a little, brokers will arrange too many clients next day.

**LAWYER 4**: (observing dissent in her facial expression) Why madam should compromise being such a high class advocate coming from America? It's our duty to bring cases to madam and she will win the cases putting strong plea before Judge Saheb. We will get our share and unitedly we will definitely leave others behind.

**ALL**: You gave approval. Now you see the result tomorrow. Meanwhile would you like to do affidavit works to meet daily expenditure.

But tomorrow never comes.

Monika's frustration grows with these insulting words, and she feels humiliated by their suggestions.

**INT. KALU AND MONIKA'S HOME - NIGHT**

The strain in Monika's professional life begins to affect her relationship with Kalu. They often argue, and tension rises.

**MONIKA:** (angrily) I can't stand the ugliness of the court environment anymore! It's weakening my confidence!

**KALU:** (defensively) I'm trying to support you, but you're pushing me away. You are getting intolerant day by day. We need to talk about this to find out an amicable solution to ever increasing domestic quarrels.

**MONIKA:** Yes, something has to be done to sort it out.

They decide to go on a three-month-long vacation to find a solution and reconnect.

**INT. MAKALU'S HOME IN CANADA - DAY - WEEKS LATER**

Kalu and Monika visit their son Makalu in Canada. They enjoy outings to idyllic places, and their relationship begins to heal. As tension eases out and confidence builds up again, Monika starts sharing her professional problems in detail with Kalu.

**MAKALU:** (concerned) I've sensed that something's not right between you two. Let's enjoy nature and forget about the worries.

They meet Makalu's Spanish friend Jennifer, who shares her acting experience and her relationship with Makalu.

**JENNIFER:** I am currently working on a small documentary in the lead role. This is the story of a dumb girl whose father does everything possible to get her voice back. As he can not afford costly voice box available in market, he invents a cheaper one. With successful transplantation of his indigenous voice box, his daughter starts speaking well.

**KALU:** Best wishes for your successful venture. If both of you like living together, then tie the wedding knot after consulting your parents.

**MONIKA:** Don't hurry. You take your own time. Many congratulations and best wishes to both of you from our side, for a wonderful happy future.

They enjoy food and coffee together, and Jennifer promises to keep them informed about her wedding plans.

**JENNIFER:** It was very nice meeting you two. How loving people you are! I'll try to come to Los Angeles with my parents. They will love to meet you and hope fully we may plan for marriage before you go back to India. Thanks for the visit.

**MAKALU:** Wow, that's great news for me too.

**INT. MAKALU'S HOME IN CANADA - NIGHT - BEFORE DEPARTURE**

Makalu talks to Monika privately, expressing his concern about her relationship with Kalu.

**MAKALU:** I don't know what's going on between you two, but everything is not the same. I just want to say that this time you must talk to me before taking any tough decision.

**MONIKA:** No son! Not such a serious problem. Petty squabbles go on between husband and wife and these are all routine things. You will understand once you get married.. Don't worry, nothing will go wrong this time.

They share a tender moment, and Monika assures Makalu that everything will be fine.

**FADE TO BLACK**

**Themes and Notes:**

**Professional Struggles:** Monika's challenges in her legal profession and the unethical practices of other lawyers highlight the difficulties she faces in her career.

**Relationship Strain:** The strain in Monika's professional life affects her relationship with Kalu. Their arguments and misunderstandings reveal the tension between them.

**Reconnection and Healing:** The vacation to Canada and the time spent with Makalu and Jennifer provide an opportunity for Kalu and Monika to reconnect and heal their relationship.

**Family Support:** Makalu's concern and support for his parents, as well as his relationship with Jennifer, add depth to the family dynamics.

**Visual and Symbolic Elements:** The visual elements include Monika's law office, their home, Makalu's home in Canada, and the idyllic places they visit. The healing power of nature symbolizes the reconnection and renewal of their relationship.

**Dialogue and Interaction:** The dialogue is filled with frustration, concern, support, and love. The interactions between the characters reveal their emotions, relationships, and intentions.

**Tone and Mood:** The tone shifts from frustration and tension to healing and reconnection. The mood is reflective and hopeful.

**Conflict and Resolution:** The conflicts in this chapter include Monika's professional struggles and the strain in her relationship with Kalu. The resolution comes through their vacation, open communication, and family support.

**Character Development:** The characters continue to evolve, with Monika facing professional challenges, Kalu showing support, and Makalu providing insight and concern.

This screenplay captures the struggles, tensions, and healing in the characters' professional and personal lives. The visual elements create a cohesive and engaging narrative, while the dialogue and interactions provide insight into the characters' emotions and relationships. The chapter concludes with a sense of hope and renewal, as the characters reconnect and look forward to a brighter future.

# Scene 44

**INT. MONIKA'S BUNGALOW - LOS ANGELES - DAY**

Camera opens up panning a grand bungalow and focuses on Monika and Kalu entering.

Monika and Kalu arrive at Monika's bungalow. They are greeted by the caretaker.

**KALU:** Sweetheart! Your face has blossomed after coming here. The old charm has returned. That's why I have suggested against the selling all these properties. It's quite soothing and nostalgic when you return back to the place where you have spent so much time.

**MONIKA:** You are far sighted, and my scope of thinking remains a bit limited. You had taken a very right decision then. Now You relax here as

I am going to nearby market to do shopping of some groceries and other items for daily use. Then I will prepare dinner.

**KALIKA**: Will it be better if we dine out alongwith shopping together?

**MONIKA**: That's nice idea! We will enjoy a romantic candle light dinner akin to dating before marriage.

**INT. RESTAURANT - NIGHT**

Monika and Kalu enjoy a romantic dinner, reminiscing about their past and celebrating their present.

**MONIKA**: I can easily feel the Warmth of conjugal life returning back at full swing between us.

**KALU**: Me too. It's because of change of place as well as being away from your professional tension demeaning your worth.

**MONIKA:** I am already anticipating the same vigor of first night when we go to bed tonight.

**KALU :** Why not! Let's start with long kiss here.

### INT. MONIKA'S BUNGALOW - VARIOUS DAYS

Monika reconnects with old associates and junior lawyers. She accepts offers for short-term legal works on their insistence. Soon she gets too busy to spare sufficient time for Kalu.

Meanwhile, Kalu explores the city, takes up gardening, and helps Monika in the kitchen. He decides to visit alone to other uncovered cities in America as when he asks Monika to come with him, she shows her inability because of predetermined professional engagement.

### INT. VARIOUS TOURIST DESTINATIONS - DAYS

Kalu travels alone, exploring new places, writing his newfound experiences in diary, and taking photographs. He reflects on his loneliness and compares the difference between temporary and indefinite separation. He also finds the benefits of not always accompanied by spouse as he freely intermingles with other tourists.

**INT. MONIKA'S BUNGALOW - DAY**

Kalu returns from his travels, and Monika teases him about his unbridled fun.

**MONIKA:** How is it that you roam freely here leaving me in the middle of the files? Your happy face is gossiping about unbridled fun.

**KALU:** This is great! The principle of you wives is to have both things my way. First refused to come with me and now complaining about unbridled fun by deliberately leaving you here.

They share a playful banter.

**INT. MONIKA'S BUNGALOW - NEXT MORNING**

Makalu, Jennifer, and her parents arrive. They get to know each other, and after sometime open up sharing details of each other's family, culture and tradition.

.

**JENNIFER'S PARENTS:** We think Makalu and Jennifer should marry each other as they have lived in for sufficient time and know each other well. The compatibility level of them sounds good. We propose a one-day event at the church and temple in the first week of the next month before you return to India.

**KALU and MONIKA:** We agree and hope Makalu and Jennifer will be comfortable with the plan.


**JENNIFER:** We are.


**MAKALU:** (to Jennifer) If it's so, why not we get engaged today evening.


**ALL :** That's nice idea! Done.

They celebrate the engagement with a small party in the evening at a local restaurant. Rings were exchanged and cake cutting done in presence of few local guests.


**INT. MONIKA'S BUNGALOW - LATER**


Monika and Kalu scrutiny the guest lists for the wedding at Los Angeles and reception at Hyderabad, India. Kalu notices Nehal's name is missing in either list.

**KALU:** Nehal's name is not there in both the lists. Has he refused to come or has it happened by mistake?

**MONIKA:** Before sending him an invitation, think with a cool head whether it would be appropriate to invite him or not.

**KALU:** We should forget past incidents. We should also remember his favour extended to us time and again instead of contemplating his wrong doings only.

**MONIKA:** You decide what would be proper. I have no personal grudge against him. So, no objection from my side.

They decide to invite Nehal.

### INT. WEDDING VENUE - DAY

The grand wedding ceremony takes place, attended by guests from India and local friends. So many indian guests coming across seven sea to just take part in wedding of their near dear impresses Jennifer and her parents a lot.

**JENNIFER:** (to Makalu and her parents) How nice people are these family members of Makalu! Now, I am looking forward with great enthusiasm to my tour to India for reception and honeymoon in Kashmir valley.


Nehal attending the wedding, expresses his gratitude.


**NEHAL:** Monika and Kalika, I am very happy that you have confirmed the survival of our old friendship by inviting me here. I would have attended only reception at Hyderabad but I had to reciprocate your kind gesture and so I decided to attend both.


He repeats his old proposal to Monika as they say goodbye.

## FADE TO BLACK

**Themes and Notes:**

**Reconnection and Rediscovery:** Monika and Kalu reconnect with old friends and rediscover their love for each other in a new setting. Monika's return to her legal work in Los Angeles also symbolizes a reconnection with her professional identity.

**Loneliness and Reflection:** Kalu's solo travels provide an opportunity for reflection on loneliness and the difference between temporary and indefinite separation.

**Celebration and Family:** The planning and celebration of Makalu and Jennifer's wedding bring together family and friends, bridging cultural differences and strengthening relationships.

**Visual and Symbolic Elements:** The visual elements include Monika's bungalow, the restaurant, various tourist destinations, and the wedding venue. The bungalow symbolizes Monika's independence and self-acquired property, while Kalu's travels symbolize his exploration of self.

**Dialogue and Interaction:** The dialogue is filled with playful banter, emotional expressions, and thoughtful reflections. The interactions between the characters reveal their emotions, relationships, and intentions.

**Tone and Mood:** The tone shifts from playful and romantic to reflective and celebratory. The mood is joyful and thoughtful.

**Conflict and Resolution:** The minor conflict regarding Nehal's invitation is resolved through understanding and forgiveness.

**Character Development:** The characters continue to evolve, with Monika reconnecting with her professional identity, Kalu exploring his feelings of loneliness, and Makalu and Jennifer planning their future together.

This screenplay captures the joy, reflection, and celebration in the characters' lives as they reconnect with old friends, plan a wedding, and explore new horizons. The visual elements create a vibrant and engaging narrative, while the dialogue and interactions provide insight into the characters' emotions and relationships. The chapter concludes with a sense of fulfillment and anticipation for the future, as the characters celebrate love, family, and friendship.

❑❑

# Scene 45

### INT. RECEPTION HALL - NIGHT

Camera opens up panning The hotel moves towards reception hall focussing on to the stage with bride and groom sitting there, then panning back to cover gathering.

The reception is in full swing. Makalu and Jennifer, the bride and groom, sitting on throne-like chairs, surrounded by guests. They struggle to connect with the continuous crowd.

**JENNIFER:** How many of these will you recognize when you meet again?

**MAKALU:** None. Don't worry, just smile with folded hands. No need to do anything more than this.

They continue to greet guests, feeling like automatic mannequins.

**INT. RECEPTION HALL - CORNER - NIGHT**

Kalu sits alone, feeling sad and remembering Sunanda. Monika is busy with guests but worried about her loneliness in near future after the function is over. She spots Nehal among the guests.

**MONIKA:** (to herself) Kalu will start going to office after 2-3 days and I will again have to either sit at home or to join same nasty dealings in local court. Should I join Nehal's office if he shifts it to Hyderabad. He will be busy in politics and hardly get time to rekindle his dead love for me. I should talk to Kalu regarding this.

She searches for Kalu and finds him sitting alone in distant corner.

**MONIKA:** What happened here sitting alone silently inconsolable? Are you missing me?

**KALU:** Yes of course! I found you busy with ladies. So I decided to sit here.

**MONIKA:** What should I do regarding Nehal's proposal regarding joining his office at Hyderabad?

**KALU :** Not a bad idea at all! It would be better to work in some private legal firm rather than wasting talent in the court waiting for clients. If you have any doubt, just try it for few days and if you don't like, give it up.

**MONIKA:** (seeing Nehal coming towards them) Then, you have a talk with him.

**NEHAL:** Hi friends! Lucky to catch lovebirds sitting away from the gathering.

**KALU:** Hi Nehal! Thanks a lot for giving your precious time to grace the occasion. How is your life going on? Quite busy with legal practice, politics and painting as well going popular now a days!

**NEHAL:** Everything fine! But very difficult to handle all these. If you can persuade Monika to take charge of my legal firm, it will be a great help to me.

**KALU:** (to Monika) Why not you are ready to help our long time friend, particularly if he is ready to shift his office here? I think, you should be considerate in dealing with his proposal.

**MONIKA:** As both of you are insisting I am ready to join but I will work only from 1 pm to 5pm and return home before you come from office.

**NEHAL:** Agreed. You will be the boss of Hyderabad office after all.

**MONIKA:** Then it's fine. You inform me when I have to join.

**NEHAL:** Many thanks to both of you. Only a friend helps a friend. It'll be done in a fortnight and I will inform you accordingly. Now allow me to leave.

Nehal departs after exchanging pleasentries.

They return to attend the reception with renewed enthusiasm.

**INT. MONIKA AND KALU'S HOME - EVENING - MONTHS LATER**

Monika returns home, furious. Kalu tries to calm her down.

**MONIKA:** He was trying to be blunt again today. I slapped him hard and showed him his status.

**KALU:** Who, my dear? First gulp a glass of water, cool down and then tell me in details what happened.

**MONIKA:** The same dirty fellow, Nehal. Initially everything was fine for eight nine months. He came to office just three times in those days and avoided any personal exchange. But for last 2-3 months, he started behaving awkwardly trying to come closer to me physically. Initially when I warned him, he apologized . But today he stooped so low that he proposed to marry him giving you divorce. He mentioned about his wealth and power and started talking evils about you and denigrating you Then I slapped him and threatened to file a case against him. I'll teach that filthy man, who shamelessly call himself your friend, a good lesson in court. I warn , you will not forgive him this time.

Learning about Nehal's inappropriate behavior Kalu supports Monika's decision to cut ties with him.

**KALU:** You have already taught him a lot of lessons. Now spit out your anger.

**MONIKA:** You still are lenient to him and that rascal compares himself with you, a gem of person. He can't deserve to be equal to your feet's dust.

**KALU:** Now spit out your anger and take sips of tea prepared by me. Today we will dine out in a good restaurant.

**MONIKA:** I have got the best husband in world. Now, I will never do any practice and create problems for you.

They go out for dinner, and Monika repeatedly vows to give up advocacy.

**INT. MONIKA AND KALU'S HOME - DAY - WEEKS LATER**

Kalu contemplates their situation and proposes a plan to balance their love, ambition, and sacrifice.

**KALU:** I want you to return to California and do justice to your profession.

**MONIKA:** No, not at all. I'll not leave you alone nor myself going back to wilderness with deafening silence worse than death.

**KALU:** I have not finished yet. After three months I will join you there taking leave from my office. Then I'll return to India and we'll live away from each other for next three months. In last three months of annual term, you will come back to India away from your practice but together with me. In this way we will spend three months each in two alternate installments of living together and staying away from each other. This way we will not get bored from each other.

Monika considers the proposal and agrees.

**MONIKA:** Thus the periodical meeting and parting will keep our romance afresh forever. A nice solution from a true loving genius!

**FADE OUT TO BLACK**

Camera focuses on to
### THE END

**Themes and Notes:**

**Balance and Compromise:** The chapter explores the delicate balance between ambition, love, sacrifice, and solitude. Kalu and Monika find a compromise that allows them to pursue their individual goals while maintaining their relationship.

**Trust and Betrayal:** Nehal's betrayal of Monika's trust leads to a breakdown in their professional relationship. Kalu's support and understanding help Monika navigate this difficult situation.

**Loneliness and Connection:** The theme of loneliness runs throughout the chapter, from Makalu and Jennifer's isolation at their reception to Kalu's memories of Sunanda and Monika's fears for the future. The characters grapple with the tension between solitude and connection, finding ways to bridge the gap.

**Character Development:** The characters continue to evolve, with Monika standing up for herself against Nehal's inappropriate advances, Kalu supporting her decisions, and both of them finding a way to balance their individual ambitions with their relationship.

**Visual and Symbolic Elements:** The visual elements include the reception hall, Monika and Kalu's home, and the dinner scene. The throne-like chairs symbolize Makalu and Jennifer's temporary status as the center of attention, while the clocks mentioned by Kalu symbolize the passage of time and the rhythm of their relationship.

**Dialogue and Interaction:** The dialogue is filled with emotion, tension, and thoughtful reflection. The interactions between the characters reveal their feelings, decisions, and the dynamics of their relationships.

**Tone and Mood:** The tone shifts from celebratory to tense, reflective, and ultimately hopeful. The mood is complex, encompassing joy, anger, contemplation, and resolution.

**Conflict and Resolution:** The conflicts include Nehal's betrayal, Monika's anger, and the tension between ambition and relationship. The resolutions come through understanding, support, and compromise.

This screenplay captures the complexities of relationships and the challenges of balancing individual goals with shared commitments. The visual elements create a rich and engaging narrative, while the dialogue and interactions provide insight into the characters' emotions and decisions. The chapter concludes with a sense of hope and resolution, as the characters find a way to navigate their individual paths while maintaining their connection.

www.ingramcontent.com/pod-product-compliance
Lightning Source LLC
LaVergne TN
LVHW091620070526
838199LV00044B/868